This book makes it so easy to find useful, realistic, and sensible answers to the most-common questions teens have about grief.

SAM HODGES IV
President of GriefShare

I hate that Clarissa and Fiona Moll had to write this book. But I am so deeply grateful they did. Their conversational tone makes this difficult material both relatable and accessible for the hurting teen, and simultaneously equips parents, church leaders, and caretakers with language and tools to help adolescents find real hope in Jesus, even in the midst of confusing, arduous losses. The Molls beautifully lead the hurting teenager to find hope in Jesus and towards emotional and spiritual health—without bypassing their grief and pain. This book is a necessary and important resource.

AUBREY SAMPSON
Pastor and author of *Big Feelings Days*, *The Louder Song*, and *Known* and cohost of the *Nothing Is Wasted* podcast

As a college missionary, I often meet students who experienced profound loss during their teen years without a guide to help them. This book is the guide they needed. Through firsthand experience and information on how grief affects our bodies and brains, Clarissa and Fiona explain grief in a way that is gentle and understandable. They point teens to gospel hope without minimizing their painful experiences and emotions. Full of self-assessments, practical tips, and plenty of resources, this is a book teens will go to over and over again, and one I will use in my ministry and with my own grieving teen.

ELISE BOROS
Campus Missionary Staff with Cru

T0281947

In *Hurt, Help, Hope*, Clarissa and Fiona Moll have created a holy space. For young people dealing with life's most massive things, here is a path towards healing. Sensitive, practical, powerful help. A true gift for parents and teens alike.

W. LEE WARREN, MD
Author of *Hope Is the First Dose* and host of *The Dr. Lee Warren Podcast*

This is the book I would have loved to have handed my teens after their dad suddenly went to heaven. Clarissa and Fiona have created an easily understandable resource tackling the issues teens navigate emotionally, physically, and socially after loss with authenticity and gospel truth. Powerful and delightfully free from pat answers, this book will become an interactive companion in teen grief. *Hurt, Help, Hope* should be on the nightstand of every teen grappling with grief.

LISA APPELO
Author of *Life Can Be Good Again: Putting Your World Back Together After It All Falls Apart* and mom to seven

HURT
HELP
HOPE

wander™
An imprint of
Tyndale House
Publishers

HURT

A REAL CONVERSATION

HELP

ABOUT TEEN GRIEF

HOPE

AND LIFE AFTER LOSS

CLARISSA MOLL & FIONA MOLL

Visit Tyndale online at tyndale.com.

Visit Clarissa Moll online at clarissamoll.com.

Tyndale and Tyndale's quill logo are registered trademarks of Tyndale House Ministries. *Wander* and the Wander logo are trademarks of Tyndale House Ministries. Wander is an imprint of Tyndale House Publishers, Carol Stream, Illinois.

For manufacturing information regarding this product, please call 1-855-277-9400.

For information about special discounts for bulk purchases, please contact Tyndale House Publishers at csresponse@tyndale.com, or call 1-855-277-9400.

Library of Congress Cataloging-in-Publication Data

A catalog record for this book is available from the Library of Congress.

ISBN 978-1-4964-8724-7

Printed in the United States of America

30	29	28	27	26	25	24
7	6	5	4	3	2	1

To Uncle Adam and Auntie Gina
A threefold cord is not quickly broken.

—C. M. AND F. M.

CONTENTS

WELCOME

Hi, I'm Fiona, and I lost my dad in a hiking accident while on vacation with my family. I was about to turn fourteen, and not only was I becoming a teenager (which God knows is hard enough), but now my life had completely changed.

On that night five years ago, my friends and I pulled into their driveway after a day at the county fair. When I saw all the cars outside, I thought they were throwing us a going-away party. It was the last day of our vacation—maybe all of our friends had come to surprise us!

I quickly noticed that something was wrong. Chaplains from the local police department stood talking to my mom. I had barely gotten out of the car when they gathered us together—my mom, my three younger siblings, and me—and gave us the worst news we had ever heard. "Your dad was hiking, and he slipped and fell. I'm sorry, but your dad has died."

This is only supposed to happen in books or movies, I thought as we all began to cry. It was the worst news, the worst time, and the worst day of my life.

The week after my dad died was crazy. My mom (Clarissa, the other author of this book) had countless phone calls to make, and family flew in from across the country. I felt like a mess physically and emotionally. It seemed as though nothing would ever be okay again. The next few years weren't easy either. My first day back at school was super awkward, the COVID-19 pandemic later shut the world down, and we moved. Twice. In two years. Life felt like a thousand terrible noises sounding all at once.

Despite all of this, I've been able to find peace over the last five years. When the noise gets too loud and I start to worry, I've learned to take hold of the promise that God has made to me.

> "For I know the plans I have for you," declares the LORD, "plans to prosper you and not to harm you, plans to give you hope and a future. Then you will call on me and come and pray to me, and I will listen to you. You will seek me and find me when you seek me with all your heart."[1]

These verses have guided me through my grief and given me peace when I felt like everything was falling apart. When I try to handle things myself, when I worry about the future, these words remind me that God has a plan. I might not know what it is, but I do know that it is for my good. He will stay near to me and listen to all I have to say. I believe he will do the same for you.

TALKING ABOUT DEATH

Our world doesn't do an awesome job teaching us about grief, death, and loss. So, if you're not sure what to think, do, or feel after the death of your person, we want you to know that's totally okay. You may know a decent amount about the deaths of famous people or deaths that you hear about on the news. You've probably watched movies where deaths occur, and you may play video games that involve death. But chances are you've never thought much about loss unless it's actually happened to you in real life.

This means that since your person died, you probably have a lot of questions. You wonder what's normal, what comes next, or what to do with the crazy feelings you have bouncing around inside of you. You wonder if God is real or even cares at all.

You may also feel like you're not sure who to ask. Maybe the death happened in your family, and you worry you'll make things worse by asking questions. Maybe the death happened outside of your family, and it seems like everybody else is moving on and you're the only one with problems. All of those unspoken feelings and unasked questions can act like a barricade of silence around you, separating you from the world and from the life you once knew (and want to live again).

We wish this book didn't exist—honestly. We wish that death didn't exist and that the pain of losing someone you love could be erased from this world. But talking less about grief and death doesn't make it go away. It only makes it harder. So we want to tell you everything we know about grief and life after loss. We want to start talking in normal voices instead of whispers about this thing that totally changes people's lives.

WHAT THIS BOOK IS (AND ISN'T)

In the years since my dad's death, my two younger brothers became teenagers, I graduated from high school, and my family of five has walked through grief together. We've wrestled with questions about God's goodness. We've had to figure out how to rebuild our lives in the absence of someone we love. We've cried and laughed and sometimes done both at the same time. Mostly, we've always tried to be 100 percent real about how hard facing death can be and how important it is that hope and honesty always walk hand in hand. We've learned a lot along the way, and we want to share it with you.

My mom and I don't have all the answers. We've learned as we've gone along, just like we know you will too. You'll figure out grief hacks that make life easier—things we've never even thought of because each person's loss is unique and sacred. (I hope you'll write and tell us your suggestions!)

While we can't know all the particular details of your relationship with your person and how his or her death has affected you, we do know this: death affects us all. Nobody escapes it. Even in its uniqueness, grief is universal. Since this is true, there's some knowledge that's pass-on-able. Your life after your person's death doesn't need to be totally uncharted territory. You can get many of your questions answered.

USING THIS BOOK

Fiona and I (Clarissa) have assembled this book so you can use it like a handbook, jumping around to the questions that feel relevant to you at the moment. (I confess, I often skip ahead to read the end of a book before I ever begin chapter 1!) If you're a person who likes to read a book cover to cover, feel free to do it! Maybe some sections of the book will never seem to apply to you, while others will become underlined and highlighted. That's okay. Maybe you'll encounter situations down the road and need to dust off this book and return to it again. That's okay too. While your grief will take a different shape over time, you'll always have its companionship on your life's journey, so grab this book whenever grief needs addressing. This book isn't something you just read. We hope it's a tool you'll be able to use to build a joyful life with grief and Jesus beside you.

As we wrote it, Fiona and I wanted to make sure that your most pressing questions were answered. Many of the questions in this book are actual topics that we discussed in our family during the early years after our loss. Others are questions we discovered through conversations that many teens were asking.

I hope that as you read this book you can imagine hanging out with Fiona and me, asking and answering questions without awkwardness and with lots of honesty. Consider us your grief friends. Research also tells us that students who go through tough experiences in their youth really benefit from one trusted flesh-and-blood adult in their lives, and we encourage you—beyond the friendship of this book—to pick out one adult in your everyday life who can be that person for you. Consider a relative, a coach, a teacher, a neighbor, or a youth leader. This dependable, trustworthy, wise adult can encourage you on days when you need some extra hope.

THE WORDS YOU NEED TO HEAR

There are so many things we hear when we're grieving. We hear a lot of "We're praying for you" and "I'm sorry for your loss." We ask ourselves, *When will this stop?* and *Will I ever be okay?* With all of these voices, it can be hard to hear the truth that God is speaking to us.[2] In the clamor of grief, we need to find a quiet place where we are able to think clearly and hear the truth of God's Word. We hope this book offers you that needed space.

I wish we could promise you that you will get all your questions answered. That you'll feel a ton better and the tightness in your chest when you think about your dead person will lift entirely. I wish we could promise you a quick fix. But we can't. However, we are convinced that Jesus can offer you perfect understanding *and* new life again. The Bible tells us in Isaiah 53:3 that Jesus was good friends with sorrow. He knew the voice of sadness and the ache and confusion of loss. Better yet, as the worship song says,

All our sickness, all our sorrows
Jesus carried up the hill.
He has walked this path before us,
He is walking with us still.[3]

At every step on your journey with grief, Jesus has promised to walk beside you. Psalm 23 describes him as the Good Shepherd who provides for his hurt and tired sheep. The book of Revelation describes him as a rider on a battle horse, a warrior called "Faithful and True."[4] You can find all kinds of companions as you figure out how to navigate your life after loss, but Jesus will always be the best friend, the one you can trust to comfort and fight for you, to tell you the truth and help point your feet toward hope.

We can have full assurance of Jesus' presence because of the cross. Through his death, Jesus paid for our sins once and for all.[5] The curse of sin that had brought death and destruction was broken. Furthermore, God's gift of new life began when Jesus rose from the grave. He not only sealed our forgiveness; he confirmed our eternal destiny. When we trust in him, resurrection life is ours too—now, as an appetizer of the great feast that awaits us when he comes again.

Not a day goes by where I (Fiona) don't miss my dad, but I have come so far from that night five years ago. I went to high school, I started two new sports, and I learned how to grow with my grief. I believe you can face life again and live joyfully too. I know we're just getting to know each other, but I want you to know how much my mom and I care about you. We want you to know how terribly sorry we are that you have to know what deep loss feels like.

We also want you to know how beloved you are in God's eyes. God delights in you, and even when the darkness feels darkest, he won't abandon you. If that's hard for you to believe, my mom and I will believe it and keep singing it for you and to you until it can become your own song of trust. The melody of God's faithfulness runs through all of creation and history. He won't fail you now.

Okay. Let's dive into your questions together.

1

IN YOUR BODY

Remember when you got "the sex talk"? You may have had a parent sit you down and give you the stark details while you sweated and squirmed a little and tried to think up excuses of how you could get away. Yeah, talking about sex and bodies can feel pretty awkward.

You may find the same thing when you start to think about your own body and its relationship to grief. Maybe you're the person who has tried to ignore your body's signs that it needs help. Maybe you haven't even been able to identify how you're feeling. No worries. We're here for you.

We're not doctors, and this chapter isn't professional medical advice. If you need that sort of care, we hope you'll seek it out. Instead, this chapter is about the crazy, all-over-the-place physical sensations that come with losing someone you love. We'll answer your questions, dispel the cringe, and, hopefully, help you feel better as you learn to navigate your life with grief.

WHY START HERE?

If grief is mostly about sadness, why start by talking about our bodies? While grief is an emotional expression that we experience after the death of a loved one, our emotions are only a part of who we are. If you've ever "felt butterflies" when a text from someone you like pings on your phone; if you've ever "felt sick to your stomach" because you were nervous about a test, you know that your emotions are intimately connected to your flesh-and-bone self.

Research tells us that our guts and our brains are wired to talk to each other all day long. Your brain tells your gut when you're having friendship troubles, and you get that sinking feeling in the pit of your stomach. Your heart tells your brain that you're excited at the pep rally as your pulse quickens in the noisy school gym. Back and forth, 24-7, your body and mind talk in endless conversation. Feelings show up in dreams at night. Hunger pangs remind you that you need to eat to stay alive even when the rest of you feels dead with sadness.

When we think about facing our grief, the emotional dimension of our loss can look totally overwhelming. From our experience (and the experiences of lots of folks we've talked to), you can start your journey with grief a little easier if you start by tending to your body first. After all, your body will take you where you want to go; and, like a car, it needs fuel and maintenance.

THE HEALING SCAR-BEARER

The Bible tells us over and over again that human bodies matter to God. In the Garden, God gently formed Adam's body from the dust of the ground and breathed his divine life into him. Adam didn't just have a body as a shell for his soul; he was a fully integrated person made in God's image. Human bodies mattered so much to God that when he came to live with his people, he took on flesh and became like us.[1]

As Christians, we take comfort knowing that Jesus experienced what it was like to live in a human body like ours. He got hungry (Mark 11:12), thirsty (John 19:28), and tired (John 4:6). Jesus experienced pain when people injured him (Matthew 27:28-29). Jesus understood physical longing and temptation (Matthew 4:1-4; Hebrews 4:15). If nobody else in your life gets how hard it is to live in your body with grief, be assured: Jesus gets it.

More than that, Jesus understands that grief will travel with you in your body for years to come. He healed people who had been sick for years (Luke 8:43-48). He befriended those with disabilities (Mark 2:1-12). Jesus knew how sorrow and loss could mark a person for life.

In one way or another, you'll be marked by your loss. Some days, grief will be quiet and almost invisible, only to show up other days in the form of a sleepless night or an upset stomach. Years from your loss, a memory of your person might bring the kind of sadness that makes you lose your appetite. Jesus gets this. He understands that we carry painful scars of hurt because he bears scars too.

After Jesus' resurrection, he walked along a road with two men who didn't recognize him. Blinded by their sorrow, these two men poured out their hearts to the risen Jesus. They told him about their Teacher, who had died a painful death. They told him about their hopes, which had been snuffed out like a candle. And when they invited Jesus in to dinner, these two men got the surprise of their lives.

With hungry bellies, they gathered around the table; and, with stunned faces, they watched as this mystery man from the road blessed the food. A man they suddenly realized they knew because he'd eaten with them so many times before (see Luke 24:13-35). Thomas, a disciple, recognized Jesus by his scars (see John 20:24-29). Death's mark became the place where Thomas could come alive again, the place where Thomas knew Jesus best.

"We bear all the ruins of the lives we've lived and the loves we've endured. What a gift to have a Savior who does the same," writes

QUIZ: LOSS AND RESTORATION

Dutch psychologists Margaret Stroebe and Henk Schut learned in their research that grieving people move back and forth between experiences that remind them of their loss and experiences that move them forward into new life.[2] Both kinds of experiences support your physical well-being as you grieve and grow. What kind of activity might you need to help you today? Take this quiz to find out!

Circle the statements below that best describe how you feel at this moment.

1. I just want to watch TikTok. I feel numb.
2. I am tired of so much sadness. I want to feel like myself again.
3. I can't believe my person is actually dead. That reality blows my mind.
4. I think journaling about my person might help me today.
5. I want my old life back.
6. Even if it makes me sad, I like to listen to music that makes me think about my person.
7. I want to cry or yell or punch something. My feelings feel really big right now.
8. I think I'm becoming a better friend. My loss has given me a new perspective on life.
9. I'm trying to adjust to life without my person, but it feels really hard.
10. I know "moving on" isn't really a thing, but I sure wish it was!

IF YOU CIRCLED MOSTLY ODD-NUMBERED RESPONSES, you might benefit from time or an activity today that allows you to feel your grief deeply. Make some space in your day to have that cry or talk to a trusted friend or just take a walk where you can move your body and let your feelings move through you. Some days with grief are really hard. It's okay to give your body what it needs.

IF YOU CIRCLED MOSTLY EVEN-NUMBERED RESPONSES, you might benefit from time or an activity today that gives you space to think about your growing life with loss. Healthy distractions like hanging out with friends or playing sports can offer you relief from grief and remind you that life is bigger than your loss. Reflect on how God is in the business of restoration and resurrection. Even in little ways, he's doing that in your life today!

author Kate Bowler.[3] We remember this as we take care of our bodies in grief. They carry important stories about who we are and what we have lost, and they hint at the resurrection that Jesus promises.

Let's dig into your questions and see how we can help.

YOUR QUESTIONS ANSWERED

I don't want to eat anymore. What should I do?

When your brain is laboring over hard news, food can be the last thing on your mind. You may be so overcome with emotion (or so zoned out) that you don't even realize your body is sending you messages that it's hungry. Your stomach may be so knotted up with anxiety or frustration or sadness that even the thought of dinner makes you nauseous. This totally makes sense. You're going through a lot right now.

It's important to distinguish between hunger and appetite. Hunger happens when your digestive system has a conversation with your nervous system; it's your body's way of expressing its need for fuel.[4] Appetite, on the other hand, is all about desire,[5] and here's where grief can make things messy. Grief can really make you lose your appetite.

Honoring your body's need for fuel while respecting your body's diminished appetite can be a delicate dance of self-kindness. However, we know that you can do it. Your physical health is important to you and those who love you.

Especially in early grief, try to eat as regularly as you can—even if you're eating a little less or feeling pickier about your menu choices than usual. Offer yourself snacks between formal mealtimes if you find you're eating less than normal. Go easy on the junk food if you notice you're turning to food for comfort. Use the BRAT diet for a few days—bananas, rice, applesauce, and toast—to help settle your stomach if you're spending a lot of uncomfortable time in the bathroom. Gentle eating eases your digestive system so you're less likely to get a bellyache.

As you commit to gentle eating, respect your grieving appetite. Lots of people bring food after the death of a loved one, but you're not required to eat what doesn't taste and smell good just to be polite. This isn't the time to pressure yourself to clean your plate. Instead, confidently select items that promote health: whole grains, fruits, veggies, and protein. Ask a trusted adult to pick up an item at the grocery store that would taste good to you. The key here is to keep fueling your body so you have the strength to face the day.

In time, as your body adjusts to your loss, you'll find that your appetite most likely begins to return. If you find you're starting to turn to food regularly for comfort or if you continue to struggle with eating, talk to a parent or school counselor for extra support.

Am I crazy or is my hair actually falling out?

You're definitely not crazy, but it may be true—you may be experiencing hair loss provoked by your grief. The medical term here is *telogen effluvium*, and it's a common occurrence after a stressful experience. When you lose a loved one, your whole body feels it, even your hair follicles.

The good news is that almost always hair loss like this stops on its own.[6] Over time, you'll see less of your hair in the drain after you shower. You'll brush your hair and find less of it in the brush.

What can you do in the meantime? Eat healthy and try to get the rest your body needs. As you care for the other parts of you, you'll reduce the stress your system is carrying, and your hair will respond.

As always, if you notice something that makes you feel uncomfortable, talk to your doctor or school nurse about it. Talking to a medical professional doesn't mean that something is going to be terribly wrong with you. Oftentimes, a conversation with a doctor can offer you the reassurance that your body is normal and doing just fine.

I'm breaking out all over. It's terrible!

After the death of your person, it's normal to experience a major acne attack. As a teenager, you already know that your body is a rush of hormones. Grief really can throw these hormones out of whack for a season. Many times, this stress shows up on your skin as zits. For the most part, these changes are temporary. As you get the rest you need, eat right, and reduce stress, your hormones will readjust. Your skin problems most likely will return to whatever has been normal for you before.

While your body is going through this upheaval, offer yourself an extra dose of compassion as you look in the mirror each day. Use these basic self-care rituals as acts of compassion for your hurting body. Your body is your friend.

- Make sure you're showering regularly and washing your face.
- Don't spend a lot of time popping zits in front of the mirror; let your skin rest.
- Drink lots of water to keep your skin hydrated.
- Apply sunscreen when you're headed out.
- Avoid oily or sweet foods that usually cause you to break out.
- After crying, take a wet washcloth and wipe your whole face. It feels good *and* it cleanses your skin.
- If someone asks how they can help, ask them to pick up an acne face wash or blemish pads at the pharmacy for you.

I'm okay during the day, but nights are hard. I can't seem to fall asleep. Help!

When I (Clarissa) was a college student, I worked at a summer camp in the White Mountains of New Hampshire. Churches and nonprofits often bused in kids from the inner city of Boston for a week in nature, and nothing made those kids more unsettled than the dark sky over the mountains at night. They were accustomed to the 24-7 lights of the city, so the thick, quiet, starlit darkness of camp made them awfully uncomfortable.

You don't need to be standing in a forest beneath the stars to find nighttime hard. If you're going, going, going all day long, nighttime may be the first chance you have to stop and actually think. The quietude of your bed may feel stifling, frightening, or just plain uneasy. Trying to sleep in an environment that makes you uncomfortable can feel impossible.

We acknowledge it—nighttime is the hardest time. You're alone in your room, the lights are off, and your mind begins to wander. Your body is tired, and in your weariness, grief starts to speak loudly. Add to that the pressure that you have to wake up tomorrow and head to school and do it all over again? No wonder you have trouble getting the rest you need!

The best way to help your body fall asleep is to give it cues. Create a little routine that you can use each night and start doing it. Turn off your phone at least thirty minutes before you plan to turn off the lights and charge it in another room. Wash your face and brush your teeth. Change into different clothes for bed. (It's surprising how psychologically helpful that can be!)

When you're fully ready for bed, take some time to relax your body and your mind. First, tighten your muscles and release them, starting with your toes and working up to the top of your head. Take a deep inhale through your nose, hold it for four counts, and exhale gently through your mouth. Then do something that you find restful, whether it's listening to music, reading a book, or journaling. Pray and then choose a neutral, happy image (a tropical beach, a basket of kittens, etc.) and allow your mind to rest on that image as you slowly fall asleep.

Is this a magic fix for your sleep problems? No. Will you need to depend on catnaps during the day to get you through the hardest days or weeks of your grief? Yes, maybe. A quick nap can be a great energy supplement. As with most of these body issues, time and self-kindness are your best friends. Care for your body while going to bed like you would put a baby to sleep.

A note on all-nighters: we know that sometimes you need to stay up late to get homework done, but when you're able, turn the lights out at a reasonable hour. Don't worry about falling asleep; simply let your body rest and relax in the dark. Grief can mess with our circadian rhythms and make us feel worn out all day long. If this is you, creating a regular lights-out/lights-on routine may help your body to start to feel more "normal" again.

OTHER HELPFUL HABITS TO SUPPORT HEALTHY SLEEP:

- **SLEEP IN A COOLER ROOM.** Research has shown that athletes get better sleep when they go to bed in cooler rooms. "Deep sleep is important for feeling refreshed and recovered the following day," says Dr. Christopher Winter, a consulting physician and sleep researcher for the MLB, NHL, and NBA.[7] If you're tossing and turning at night, consider lowering your bedroom's thermostat, wearing lighter clothing, or replacing that down comforter with a more breathable cotton quilt.
- **USE ESSENTIAL OILS.** Essential oils are extracted from plants and used for a variety of different purposes. Some folks use them for natural healing remedies. Others use them to promote relaxation. If you want to turn your bedroom into an oasis of calm, consider purchasing an essential oil diffuser, or simply grab an essential oil like lavender or chamomile and place a drop or two on your pillowcase. Be sure to read the instructions on the bottle (many oils shouldn't be placed directly on the skin or ingested) and be aware of allergies if you have them.

- **GRAB A NIGHT-LIGHT.** Yes, I know you put away your Lightning McQueen night-light years ago. Maybe it's time to pull it out of the drawer again. While blue and white light can make it hard to sleep, the gentle glow of a small night-light can offer quiet reassurance when the rest of your room is dark. If being in the darkness makes you uncomfortable or makes your grief as big as that monster under the bed, go ahead and turn on a little light. As you pop your night-light into the outlet, remember this verse: "O LORD, you light my lamp. My God turns my darkness into light."[8]

- **SNUGGLE WITH A STUFFIE.** Again, you might think it's stuff for little kids, but a stuffed animal can be a great snuggle partner at night. If nighttime has you really missing your person, grab a stuffie and give it a big hug. Sleep back-to-back with it, hold it in your arms as you rest, or keep it resting beside your face on your pillow as you close your eyes. I think you might be surprised how much less alone a stuffed animal can make you feel.

My mind wanders a lot. Do other people have trouble concentrating?

If you've lost track of time, forgotten what day it is, or misplaced your phone and can't remember where you put it, you might have what bereaved people call "grief brain." This brain fogginess is a normal occurrence after someone has experienced loss. Despite that, it can be scary when you forget to do simple tasks or when you zone out during classes and don't know why it's happening.

Grief brain is a survival response that eliminates stressors and allows your brain to focus on keeping you afloat. After a traumatic event, our brains need time to regain their footing in daily life before they can start to process everything that has happened.[9] It's just like learning the alphabet before you can start to read a book. In grief, our

WHEN YOU NEED EXTRA HELP

There's a lot that's within the range of normal when it comes to grief. Sleepless nights, sleepy days. No appetite and junk-food-only cravings. However, for most people, the crazy disruption to your regular habits eventually settles down, and your stomach and brain will find their way back to feeling more familiar.

Sometimes, though, your body might need extra help. If your body's aches and pains don't go away with time and gentle stretching or yoga, it might be helpful to talk with your doctor. If your lack of sleep (or abundance of it!) is becoming disruptive to your life, a professional can help you get restorative rest. And if controlling your diet or comfort eating becomes essential to coping, reach out to a trusted adult who can help you get the care you need.

Many people's bodies adjust to life after loss just fine, but some bodies need a little extra support. Thankfully, doctors and other professionals have seen it all. Your honesty about your body won't surprise them, and your willingness to bravely ask for help will impress them with your maturity and wisdom.

If you are struggling with an eating disorder or another crisis, turn to the appendix on page 123 for numbers you can call or text that provide 24-7 care and support.

brains need to focus on the basic skills of daily living before we can begin to sort out everything else. If you overload the circuits, your brain starts to smoke! This explains why you can remember to go to the bathroom, but you can't remember where you put your keys.

The good news is that grief brain happens to a lot of people. You're not going insane. You're not losing your mind. It's frustrating if you start forgetting your homework or accidentally bleach a whole load of laundry. (That happened here!) But be patient with yourself. As time passes, your grief brain will be able to handle more, and life will become less foggy and confused. Until then, move a little more slowly, be a little more careful, avoid loud or crowded spaces where it's hard to think, and give yourself extra grace when you forget important details.

I am exhausted and overwhelmed. Life feels too fast and loud. How can I slow it down?

We're not surprised that life feels noisier for you than usual. Grief affects all of our senses—taste, sight, smell, touch, and, yes, even hearing. The world can feel like sensory overload when your brain and heart are trying to process the death of your person. You may feel like you're on a crazy carnival ride that's spinning and flashing or like you're wandering through a hall of mirrors where all of life looks more than a little bit distorted.

There are all sorts of ways to "slow down" your life, and some of them aren't healthy. Alcohol and drugs may hold immediate appeal because of their promise to chill you out, but their dark sides will only serve to make your grief worse. Escaping your life or your emotions through numbing video games or endless phone scrolling won't do the trick either. Your brain needs something more than a distraction or a sedative. It needs real healing and relief.

If you're feeling overwhelmed in a sensory way, first, step aside from your busy schedule. Take a temporary break from sports practice or a mental health day from an extracurricular commitment. Create some white space in your calendar. It doesn't need to be for forever, just until you're feeling less overwhelmed.

Next, consider making a comfort space in your room where your senses can relax. Montessori schools intentionally create quiet classrooms with very little on the walls to offer students a mentally relaxing space to focus. In the same way, consider clearing away extra clutter in your room so that your space reflects the spaciousness you need in your inner life. Turn off the overhead light, grab a bedside lamp, and invite ambient lighting to bring a restful vibe into your room. Make a nest with blankets and pillows where you can settle in and feel the physical comfort of soft and cozy touch.

Once you've made your own comfort space, consider cutting down on your use of noise as a distraction. Say goodbye to social media and let your brain rest from the scroll. Choose music that soothes your spirit instead of hyping you up. Step outside and experience the peace of nature. Whether you do these things as temporary fixes or they become enjoyable habits, we suspect you'll start to feel your world slow down just a little bit more.

I feel achy all over, and I don't want to move. Am I okay?

During the Civil War, many soldiers endured amputations of their limbs in an effort to help them survive injuries they'd suffered on the battlefield. Some men went to war with two legs but came home with only one. In one story, a fictional soldier named George Dedlow (based on real-life patients a Civil War doctor encountered), was left with no limbs at all, only phantom pains that existed where his arms and legs had been.[10] The ache of what was absent never left his body.

While you may not experience the phantom pains of a lost limb, you've experienced your own amputation of sorts. You've lost the living, breathing connection with someone you love. C. S. Lewis lamented as much in his book *A Grief Observed*, describing the death of his wife as an amputation.[11] As you're learning to carry grief around in your body, it makes sense that you might feel achy, tired, and resistant to move around much.

Undefined aches and pains are a normal part of grief, and it's okay to feel the way you do. Your low energy level is natural too. Grief won't always feel this way in your body; but while it does, go gentle. Sometimes aches and pains are caused by muscle tightness; grief and the changes that have come with your loss can definitely

8 WAYS TO HELP YOUR BODY ADJUST TO GRIEF

1. **HYDRATE!** Grief is a marathon, and all marathoners know you need water to survive! Fill up your water bottle before you go to school and try to drink it down to empty by the end of the day. Hydration supports both physical and emotional health by warding off headaches, tiredness, and difficulty focusing in school.

2. **AVOID THE HIGHS AND LOWS.** We all love a sugar high, but the crash sure hurts. As you work to gently nourish your body, avoid foods and drinks that put your body on a roller coaster. Soda, coffee, and energy drinks might give you the oomph to push through the day, but they'll leave you empty when their energy has run its course. Love your body by being mindful of the things you fuel it with.

3. **DOODLE.** Whether you're an artist or not, research tells us that doodling actually offers stress relief. This seemingly mindless activity can help us "find lost puzzle pieces of memories, bringing them to the present, and making the picture of our lives more whole again."[12] So go ahead, draw in the margins of your AP History notes or on scrap paper you keep beside your bed. Give your brain a rest.

4. **POP IN YOUR AIRPODS.** Music can offer great stress relief and comfort during difficult times. One study identified soothing music as a significant help for adults who wanted a good night's sleep. After listening to just forty-five minutes of peaceful music a day for three weeks, people reported that they slept better and longer than they had before![13] As your day winds down, or when you need some stress reduction, cue up a peaceful playlist and let the music help you unwind.

5. **REACH FOR THE SKY.** Any sports coach will tell you that stretching is a vital part of training for athletes. It's also a really good practice for grieving people. As you learn to live with your loss, start each morning with a simple stretching routine to gently move your body. Sitting on the edge of your bed, stretch your arms straight above your head. Inhale and hold for four counts. Gently exhale and slowly move your

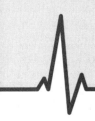

outstretched arms like a ballet dancer down to your lap again. Repeat two more times and let your body feel the expansiveness of the motion.

6. RUN, WALK, OR PUNCH SOMETHING. Movement can be a metaphor for how we move through and with grief. Do you wish you could just run away from your problems? Take a jog around your block instead. Envision stepping away from your sadness at your front door and breathe in the fresh air on a walk to the library. Too cold to be outside? Wrap a bunch of pillows in your comforter and punch the living daylights out of your frustration or anger. Thinking of movement as emotional action can allow us to channel our body's energy into profitable activity. Always remember that movement should serve to further heal your body, not hurt it. Don't engage in dangerous activities that could only make things worse.

7. LAUGH OUT LOUD. The Mayo Clinic tells us that laughter releases endorphins (happy brain chemicals) and helps you feel more relaxed.[14] It can even make your body better able to fight sickness.[15] Do your body a favor and chuckle, even if you're not feeling particularly happy. Watch a YouTube video of your favorite comedian. Fake laugh with a friend until your silliness starts to actually be funny. It matters less what you're laughing at than that your body's getting the exercise and release it needs.

8. CREATE QUIET. Quiet can feel overwhelming when you're grieving. Alone with your thoughts, your mind can wander into sad or dark places. It's easy to want to fill the emptiness with noise, to push away silence that makes space for memories. However, quiet is vital for our body's renewal. Science tells us that silence can cause our brains to grow, literally renewing our minds.[16] As you're able, create space in your day for quiet. Put away your phone and turn off the TV, and let quietness settle like a soft blanket over your body.

make you tense up. For now, consider stepping down from vigorous exercise, and try something a little easier. Instead of sprinting, jog. Yoga and stretching can help lengthen your muscles, alleviate aches, and infuse your body with softer energy that enables you to make it through the day.

All of self-care in grief is a delicate dance of leaning in and letting go. Some days, lean in and do the hard work of movement even when you don't want to. Other days, listen to your body and let go—rest, limit your movement, and let yourself repair. If you begin to experience chronic or intense pain, definitely talk to your doctor or a physical therapist.

All of a sudden, I feel a lot older. Do I actually look different?

When you encounter death as a teenager, it can seem like you've had to grow up overnight. You know more than a lot of your peers know, you've seen more than they've seen, and you've experienced heartache that they've only watched in movies. Unfortunately, you know now what it means to live as an adult in a broken world.

With all this new knowledge, it can feel like you've jumped from being a teenager to being middle-aged. Stuff you once enjoyed might seem trivial now, and when you look in the mirror, you might actually think you look older. Thankfully, you're still you. You can learn to love the person you're becoming even though the process is hard. You aren't older, but you may definitely be wiser.

Since your loss, you might discover that you act older now. Silly things don't make you laugh in the same way, or activities you once enjoyed don't spark the same joy. All of this is normal as grief becomes your companion. But here's an equally surprising thing: grief also has the capacity to make you feel young again.

You might look in the mirror and see a person who carries the weight of years. You might also discover that grief has a way of

PRAYER AND SCRIPTURE

God, I feel my loss everywhere. Sometimes it hurts so much I feel numb. Please renew my body so that I can face this day. Give me the energy I need and the moments of rest I crave. You made my body, and you called it good. I trust that you will carry me gently now. Amen.

> LORD, be kind to me. I am sick and weak. Heal me, LORD! My bones are shaking. I am trembling all over.... I cried to you all night. My pillow is soaked; my bed is dripping wet from my tears ... my eyes are worn out from crying.
> PSALM 6:2-3,6-7, ERV

> Jesus said, "Come to me, all of you who are weary and carry heavy burdens, and I will give you rest. Take my yoke upon you. Let me teach you, because I am humble and gentle at heart, and you will find rest for your souls."
> MATTHEW 11:28-29, NLT

renewing your interest in the little things in life. Before, you might have thought swinging on swings was for little kids. Now, you relish in their simple pleasure. Before, you might have smiled sweetly as a child picked dandelions along the sidewalk. Now, you find yourself bending down to grab one too—to smell it and take in its yellow cheerfulness.

Grief is a state of body *and* a state of mind. As you learn to live with grief, it will be important to "act your age" as much as you can, remembering that while loss has given you wisdom beyond your years, you're still in a young body with a young mind, living a life full of possibility and promise. God isn't done with you yet!

I'm tempted to drink or vape. Wouldn't that make me feel a little better?

We've talked a little bit about the numbing attraction of addictive substances and how they're not helpful in grief. But escaping from your problems isn't the only reason you may want to turn to nicotine, drugs, or alcohol. Sometimes you just want to fit in.

Losing a person you love can make you feel like you're the elephant in the room—the big, sad thing that nobody wants to talk to or talk about. Grief can bring with it isolation, and marijuana, alcohol, or vaping can promise a social acceptance that makes all of that isolation go away. Unfortunately, those are empty promises. On the other side of substance use is always more sadness. If you're tempted to drink or vape or use drugs, don't do it.

It's important to be especially protective of your body after loss. It's equally important to be protective of your heart. As you consider what you put into your body, ask yourself whether the choices you're making for your body are choices that truly comfort your heart as well. Are you looking for a quick fix or an easy out from the awkwardness of your situation? Or are you willing to look for real solutions that offer physical relief and long-term health? If you're not sure you're making a wise decision, ask a trusted adult like a coach or teacher for their feedback. They know what you're going through, and they will understand that the struggle is real.

I want to have sex. I just want to feel close to someone. Yes or no?

Whether or not you had the impulse to have sex before, it might surprise you that grief increases your desire for physical intimacy. We don't talk about this much, but sexual arousal and desire can be normal experiences after loss. The question for you as a teenager is, of course, what do you do with these feelings?

We believe that healthy sexual relationships are for marriage only, so we won't encourage you to act on your desires. However, it isn't only our Christian sexual ethic that makes us offer that advice. Practically speaking, bereavement just isn't the right time to make big decisions about your sexuality and sexual practices. Sexual intimacy brings with

IN THEIR OWN WORDS: LIBBY'S STORY

When I was eight years old, my friend and classmate died suddenly from early onset leukemia. I was shocked, scared, and sad. Just days earlier, we were playing, and life was normal. This was my first experience with death, and losing a good friend was traumatizing. I could not believe this could happen to someone my age.

While I was too young to recognize it at the time, it had a huge impact on me physically and emotionally. I started having stomachaches and losing my hair. I had nightmares and could not sleep alone in my room for months. I would get very anxious whenever someone I loved was not feeling well.

My mom, who has experience with grief, connected me to a child bereavement program, and I started grief therapy. The therapist helped me process what happened to my friend and helped me connect my fears to reality. I was able to reflect on our friendship, and I experienced some healing through these sessions. I remember feeling comfort knowing she was in heaven but sad that she was gone. I think her loss has shaped me in many ways. Since her death, I have a great deal of sympathy for others who are going through grief.

—Libby, age 17, whose friend died nine years prior

it all kinds of complexities that are best addressed when you're not going through big, difficult things. We'd offer adults the same exact advice.

Loss can make us feel lonely and vulnerable in all kinds of ways. Add to that the hormones of adolescence, and you can have a perfect mix of sexual feelings that seem too big to ignore. Rather than turn to sexual activity, masturbation, or pornography, we encourage you to turn to Jesus instead. Lay your desires before him in honesty; he won't judge you or condemn you for how you feel. Talk to God about the longings that you experience in your body, then make a plan to avoid temptation and fill your life with healthy, life-giving activities that will support you through this challenging phase of your grief journey. As a helpful support, tell a trusted adult about your struggles so you have someone to encourage you toward what is right.

IN THEIR OWN WORDS: MAC'S STORY

After my dad passed away, my mom and brothers constantly expressed their emotions—sadness, anger, bitterness, and more—but I resolved that I wouldn't be like *that*. I wanted to be tougher, stronger, and steadier, and I thought that meant I could never show my emotions. It also meant I didn't like to talk or even think about my dad, because that might stir up feelings I didn't want to feel (but then I'd feel guilty for not remembering him more)! So I distracted myself by trying to be like my dad in school and sports (he excelled in both), and I curated an image of the "good guy" who went to youth group, played varsity sports, and was headed to a good college. While there is no one way to grieve, I wish I'd known that grief isn't a one-time thing that I'd get over but a lifelong process.

—Mac, age 26, reflecting on the death of his father when he was 13

2
NUTS & BOLTS

Last summer, our family took a road trip to Great Smoky Mountains National Park. We hiked and saw gorgeous scenery, but perhaps the most fun part of our time was playing around in a mountain stream on a hot afternoon.

After a picnic lunch on the bank, we took off our shoes and stepped into the water. The cold mountain stream made our toes tingle, but it wasn't long until we were splashing each other and wading across to the other side. Settling into quiet activity, my brothers started moving stones to divert little currents of the stream. No matter how many stones they stacked or piled, though, the water always seemed to get through. It was pretty clear: you couldn't easily stop a river from running.

The death of your person is like a giant rock dropped into the stream of your life. Everything was flowing normally (or as normally as it ever did!), but now a huge obstacle is diverting the current. But here's the thing—your loss doesn't actually stop life from moving forward. Somehow life finds ways to keep flowing around the rock loss has dumped into your life.

One of the hardest parts of losing someone you love is that realization. Life may keep going, but you don't always know how to go along with it. Sometimes you don't even care if it leaves you behind. After your person dies, you still have to go to school. You have to report to work on the weekends. Holidays, birthdays, and special events keep showing up on the calendar. That river of life keeps flowing, and we don't want you to drown in the details.

Jesus told his followers in Luke 12 that every hair on their heads was numbered. He told them that God noticed when sparrows fell. He assured his listeners that God dressed the grass of the field and fed the birds of the air. Clearly, God cares about details. God cares about *your* details.

This section is about how to handle all those details that make the river of life feel like it's running swiftly over you. Life may call you to keep flowing along, but you're not caught in the eddies of chance. You're carried in the current of God's powerful and everlasting love for you. Over time and with experience, you'll get used to the river again and find your way toward a life you can love.

YOUR QUESTIONS ANSWERED

I'm not ready to go back to school. What should I do?

The environment of school is a busy one. There's rarely a quiet moment, and the hustle and bustle of classes can quickly feel overwhelming when your mind is somewhere else. Add to that the load of classroom discussions, homework assignments, sports schedules, and the like, and it's no surprise that you might feel like you just can't go back. School is a fast-moving stream, where learning builds upon other learning. If you get lost or behind, it can feel like you'll never be able to catch up.

When you layer on the topics that you may face in and outside of the classroom, your head *and* your heart are probably aching. If your person died of cancer, a science class about the human body may feel too tender. If you've lost a friend from school, sitting in a classroom with his or her empty chair may cause sharply painful reminders of your person's absence. If violence happened at your school, it may feel scary to even go back into the building. Some students may want to talk a lot about what happened to your person; others might act as though nothing ever occurred.

As a middle school teacher, I (Clarissa) am convinced that communication is the most important part of figuring out how to manage school when you're grieving. Talk to your parent or guardian to let them know that school feels overwhelming. Talk to your school counselor to let him or her know you're struggling. Pop into your principal's office (yup, for real!), and explain how hard it is to be in the building when you're carrying something so heavy.

After your school support team is alerted to your needs, together you can build a plan. Could you have extended time on the next few tests while your brain is in a fog? Could you listen to audiobooks instead of doing the regular reading? Might it be possible to adjust writing or literature assignments to avoid topics that touch painful memories in your life? Could you add an extra study hall to give yourself some mental space in the busyness of the school day?

Good educators are committed to helping their students succeed, and I'm convinced you can get the support you need. In most cases, the first and most important step is to reach out and tell someone you're hurting.

FUNERALS 101

Funerals bring up a lot of emotions, which may make you ask whether or not you want to go. It definitely seems easier to escape the hard memories, possibly awkward interactions, and finality of your loved person's death. However, funerals are a very important part of grieving. They give you a chance to say goodbye, and they offer you an opportunity to connect with others who are grieving the same person. If you weren't present when your person died, you may feel like you never got an opportunity to officially say goodbye. Or maybe your last interaction didn't end well. Attending the funeral is an important way to give closure to the earthbound part of your relationship.

Funerals also offer the chance to make connections with other people who were close to your person. Funerals are a sad time of grief but also a time of sharing happy memories. For example, at my dad's funeral, I (Fiona) really enjoyed being able to hear stories of him from people I never would have met otherwise.

The Lingo

The word *funeral* often encompasses a few different parts of corporate grieving rituals. Here's a quick vocabulary list so you'll know what the adults around you are talking about.

- **THE WAKE.** A wake or "viewing" occurs most often at a funeral home (or in a person's home, depending on your culture). Here, the body of the person is laid out in a casket for visitors literally to view as they say their goodbyes. The body is embalmed (preserved by an undertaker), so your person will and won't look the same as when he or she was alive. Most people say that their deceased person looked peaceful and a little like a wax museum figure. Sometimes families opt to have a partial viewing in which only the person's face and upper body are visible in the casket. It's okay to touch your person (or not). It's also okay to opt not to view the body. Often, the family of the deceased greets visitors at the wake, so if you are part of the family, be prepared for folks to talk with you. If you're a friend of the deceased, you can arrive, share your condolences, and linger as long as you feel comfortable.

- **THE FUNERAL.** The funeral is a church service in which the deceased person's body may or may not be present in a casket at the front of the church. Funeral services traditionally include prayers, songs, and a brief message from a pastor or priest. Eulogies, literally "good words," are spoken about the person who has died. A Christian funeral focuses both on the deceased person and the hope we have because of Jesus' death and resurrection.
- **THE MEMORIAL SERVICE.** A memorial service or celebration of life may include some elements of a funeral, but the primary focus of a memorial service is to remember the person who has died. Memorial services are sometimes somber, but more often they include celebratory elements. Guests might be asked to wear a color the deceased person liked or share a happy memory.
- **THE BURIAL.** A burial or committal service is a brief service that occurs in the cemetery. The deceased person's body is offered to God for safekeeping until the resurrection. Family and friends gather around a hole that has been cut in the ground, and the box of cremated remains or casket is lowered into it at the end of the service. At a burial, you may be invited to place a flower on the casket or toss a shovelful of soil over the box. Burials are usually attended by a smaller group of people than funerals and memorial services.

How do I survive this?

Funerals can seem like a challenging balancing act of your own intense emotions, pushy relatives, and much more. It is hard to find peace and quiet among all that hustle and bustle. Two things that we found helpful were having a quiet place to escape to and a friend who stuck with us the whole time.

When we were planning the funeral, we designated a special room that was only for us so that we had somewhere private to go if we needed to escape from everything outside. If we were feeling overwhelmed by our emotions or all the people, we could feel free to stay there. In a similar way, when you go to the funeral, find a spot where you can be alone when you need to. Sit in the back of the church. Locate a quiet spot just outside the front door. Slip into a bathroom stall and take a rest. You don't need to feel guilty for not wanting to socialize. Everyone's grief looks different.

After you find a quiet place where you can spend time, find someone you can hang out with. We each had a friend who stuck with us even when we were talking with relatives or other friends. We could signal quietly to this person if we needed a break, or we could simply link arms for that reassuring physical presence. A friend or trusted adult is a wonderful companion as you process emotions you are feeling in the moment, or just a great sidekick to help get you out of conversations that feel too personal.

What if I can't get there?

Sometimes the person we love dies far away from us. You may not be able to attend the funeral service or visit the graveside. While some families choose to livestream funeral services, many prefer a more intimate screen-free experience. This can make it tough when you're grieving from a distance.

If you're far but still want to be involved, consider these simple ideas to help you feel included.

* Set an alarm on your phone to pray as the funeral begins. Know that you're joining your heart with others to pray for comfort and to remember God's promise of resurrection.
* Create your own little memorial with items you have in your room on the day of the memorial service far away. Place a picture of your person or gift they gave you in a special place so that you can remember your person as you move about your day.
* Share a story about your person on the day of his or her celebration of life. Find a friend and let them know this is a big day for you and remembering helps you grieve. Share something that makes you laugh or smile.

My dad is buried across the country from where we currently live. The only time we get to visit his grave is during our once-a-year trip to Washington. Depending on the circumstances, it can be hard to visit your person whenever you want. Your loved one might be buried far away. Their family might keep their cremation urn at their house, or their ashes might be scattered somewhere. In each of these situations, it will be helpful for you to find a place or activity where you can remember them. Sit in the same booth at a restaurant you frequented together. Take a bike ride on a path you loved to walk side by side. A space or activity can be your own personal marker when you can't get to a grave to grieve.

I don't want to wear my old clothes anymore. They feel like the old me. What can I do?

We express ourselves through the clothes we wear, and your wardrobe can be a helpful way of showing the changes you feel. While it's probably not practical or affordable to toss all of your clothes and create a totally new wardrobe, consider assigning yourself a grief outfit for those days when you really need to embody your grief.

Many people wear black to funerals or a special color like white or light blue. This is actually nothing new. For millennia, bereaved people have dressed differently after the death of a loved one. Why? Because grief marks us as different, and it's helpful to have outward signs to show others that we need care, compassion, and sympathy.

If you want to dress differently, go ahead. Does a particular color remind you of your person? Choose items from your current wardrobe that feature that color and wear it with intention. Does black help to signify the sadness you're experiencing? Wear it on days that are particularly hard and explain to your friends or a trusted adult why you're making that choice. Does a shirt or sweatshirt carry a painful memory? Go ahead and stick it under your bed for a while so you don't need to see it every time you open your dresser drawer.

Many professional athletes wear a patch on their uniforms or an armband in remembrance of a player who has died. You can do something like that too. A hat from a sports team you followed together, a bracelet that your person gave you, even a pair of your sneakers that you designate as your "grief shoes" can help you express your loss in a physical way.

After Fiona's dad died, I (Clarissa) chose to wear black for a few months. Every time I went out, I wore one of the four black shirts I owned. Whether or not anybody else understood what I was doing (wearing black is pretty normal now), it was meaningful to *me*. Over time something kind of amazing happened. I got sick of wearing those shirts. I wanted to wear my regular stuff again. That's when I knew that my grief was changing shape. My sadness wasn't over—not even close—but something inside of me was growing again, and my limited black wardrobe just didn't fit right anymore.

As you figure out what clothes help you to express your grief and the changes that have come into your life because of loss, I trust that you'll know what to wear and when, just like I have. Whether you share your *why* with others or keep it in your heart, finding ways to put on (and take off) your grief will help you express the feelings that seem to defy words.

I have all these new responsibilities at home, and I hate it. Help!

Loss can turn your household upside down, and new responsibilities are the first signal that things have changed. Normal life rhythms are often disrupted immediately after a death, and you may be called upon to take up some chores or tasks that you didn't have before to help your family make it through the toughest season of loss. As much as you're able, be a team player and contribute where you can.

There is an important distinction, though, between responsibilities that are taken on for a season and those that become a permanent part of your routine. Multiple research studies detail the dangers of kids growing up too fast by taking on adult responsibilities like feeding their families every meal or putting their siblings to bed. If you're starting to feel the emotional weight of the responsibilities you have at home, talk to a parent or trusted adult about your concerns. Together you can devise a plan to do the tasks that are expected of a student your age while leaving the adult work to adults.

My family is fighting. People don't want to talk to each other anymore. What should I do?

Death often exposes conflict in families. Your person might have been a finger in the dam of a lot of family issues that are now arising in their

ACTIVITY: WHO ARE MY PEOPLE?

Grief can feel really lonely, but you don't need to go it alone. Chances are, there's somebody you already know who can offer you support and companionship as you experience grief's hardest days.

Fill in this diagram with the names of people who fit the various circles of support you need to survive and thrive again. If it's helpful, beside the names jot down what that person is good at ("listening," "texting back right away," "making me laugh," etc.).

Take a picture of your completed diagram and keep it on your phone for those days when you really need a supportive connection. You're building your own support team! (Keep in mind, too, that some people move into different circles of support over time. Someone close may drift away, or someone who was just an acquaintance can become a dear friend!)

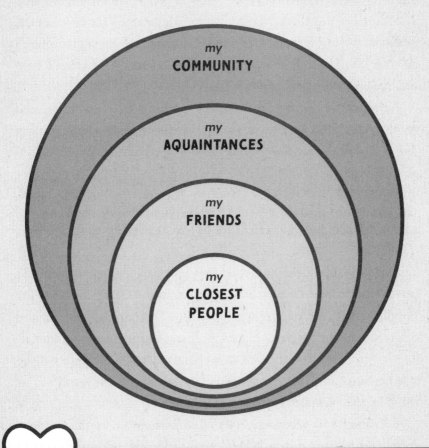

my
COMMUNITY

my
AQUAINTANCES

my
FRIENDS

my
**CLOSEST
PEOPLE**

absence. Family members might persuade you to take their side or end up doing things that hurt you. Relationships that you hoped would sustain you can get messy, uncomfortable, or downright unbearable.

In these situations, be especially intentional about boundaries. You are not a middleman or go-between in arguments. You don't serve as a buffer between feuding relatives. You are not a pawn in someone else's manipulative game. You are a grieving family member too! It's all right to say, "Please leave me out of this!"

If you're able to maintain a healthy relationship with people in your family, you may still need to avoid topics or situations that cause tension. Maybe that means you keep in touch via phone but stop attending get-togethers. Maybe that means you look for new, neutral places of common ground on which to relate. If you're not able to do this, it's okay to grieve and pray. God knows the additional pain these relationship problems are causing.

As much as you are able, respect the boundaries of others and enforce your own. As always, find an adult you trust whom you can talk to about the situation and who can give unbiased and reasonable advice.

Our vacation got canceled. I know it's probably small to some people, but it feels huge to me. Is it okay to feel this frustrated?

Yes! We actually understand well how you feel, because we lost our person in the middle of our family's vacation. Death canceled the rest of our trip, ended happy summertime visiting with friends, and replaced it all with funeral planning. It was terrible, sad, and incredibly frustrating. So don't worry, we won't tell you, "There will be another vacation." Even if there is (and there probably will be), it won't be *this* vacation. It won't be the same.

Canceled and rearranged plans unfortunately are a common accompaniment to death. Whether you've lost the person who drove you to sports practice or you have to miss the big school concert to travel to a funeral in another state, life gets really disrupted after someone dies. While we know that we always should hold our plans loosely, death reminds us in big bold letters that we're not in control of the calendar. It's a truth nobody really wants to hear.

First, tell God how you feel about your canceled plans. In reality, he's the one who designs the calendar. Psalm 139 tells us that all of our days were written in God's planner before one of them had ever come to be, and Proverbs 19 reminds us that while we make plans, God is the one who orders our days.[1] This may be frustrating to hear when something you've hoped and planned for doesn't work out, but these truths can also offer you a glimmer of hope in the midst of disappointment. God is in charge, and he understands the things you've lost.

Second, look for alternatives. Your vacation has been canceled, but could you plan a small staycation in your home with your family? Your staycation might include a special meal you make or a game night or a daily walk around the block. You could be an armchair traveler and watch a documentary of an exotic location you'd someday love to visit together. None of these are replacements for what you lost, but they do offer you the opportunity to connect with the spirit of every good family vacation—time spent playing, laughing, and just being together.

Every time I get on the playing field, I think of my person. How do I handle games, recitals, plays—all the things?

After your person dies, it can be hard to return to certain places, especially when you know that person will be missing from them. If your parent used to cheer you on from the sidelines, the soccer field may feel like an impossible place to return to. If your sibling or friend stood beside you in choir or in the concert band, you might feel like you never want to sing or play another note on that stage. Their absence taints all the happy memories of that space. Their death sucks all the oxygen out of the room or turns the field to an expanse of disappointment.

At first glance, you might think you have two choices: shoulder through and show up or never return. However, we'd like to offer you a gentler alternative to these two cold absolutes. Rather than all-or-nothing thinking, we invite you to explore the gray area in between. What might be possible if you could meet these places for the first time again?

When returning to an activity or place that is filled with memories or meaning, we encourage you to go slow—extra slow, in fact—as you let the new you adjust to this new-old space. Whether you like it or not, you're engaging in an experience and a place that is both new and old for you. New because you're not the person you were before, and you bring new experiences to it. Old because this place or experience is still filled with memories. This complicated reintroduction is going to take time.

We don't recommend the Polar Plunge method for returning to activities and places that might bring pain. Instead, try easing yourself back in the way you'd do if you were stepping into a cold pool or steaming hot tub. Take one step at a time. This might look like visiting the field alone without your team before practices start to give space for the emotions that might bubble up. It might mean sitting on the gym bleachers and closing your eyes, remembering events past and breathing in the smells of the room that conjure up memories. It might mean attending a school concert as an audience member before you decide to rejoin the choir on stage.

However you choose to slowly reengage with these activities and places, be sure to give yourself space—space to interact at your own pace, space to let emotions arise if they need to, and space to leave if the experience feels too intense. As you engage in this gentle "exposure therapy," you're creating a safe space for your body, mind, and heart to reintegrate into the new-old life that you're going to be living without your person. Some people may need only one or two gentle engagements to reacclimate, while others may need an extended period of time. What's most important is the rhythm of engagement and rest as you make forward motion toward finding your place again in these spaces.

Everybody is handing out my person's belongings, and I want something. Is it rude to ask?

It's definitely not rude to ask! In fact, we encourage you to ask. Children and teenagers possess fewer concrete memories than do their adult co-grievers, and belongings like a sweater, figurine, or ball cap can be a tangible anchor to the memory of the person who has died. After a loved one dies, it's especially important for young people to be given the opportunity to (literally) hold on to memories of their person.

Giving away a person's belongings is a very sensitive process, even for adults. Many adults struggle to know what to do with these belongings, and the process of actually distributing them might take longer than you'd like. As much as you can, be patient with the process. Verbalize your desire to have a special item that belonged to your person. Write it down as a helpful reminder to the person who is distributing items. Finally, follow up if you don't hear anything from that person. Keep in mind that more than one person may desire the item that's your favorite, so try to offer two or three options that would work for you.

As you wait and when you receive an item—and even if you're refused—remember that a person's belongings aren't equal to the person himself. You don't have less of your grandpa because you don't have his pocket watch. You don't love your friend less if you don't have the special book you two enjoyed together. A person's belongings are tokens of remembrance. If you aren't able to receive one, you are no less loved and your love is no less important to the person you lost.

I'm worried about my parents and money. Should I help out?

We love to know how much you care about your family. Money worries are common, but financial issues are often more complex than what we see on the outside. Because of this, we encourage you to release your fears about your family's money situation and trust that your parents are going to make good decisions.

If you know that money is tight, do what you can to be a good steward of what you have. Turn off the lights when you leave the room. Don't waste food. Take good care of your clothes and shoes. You can offer to get a job to help out, but be prepared for your parents to say no. It's not that they don't want your help; it's more likely that they know the situation is complicated and they want you to just enjoy being a kid. Receive that as a gift of love and let them know how much you appreciate them.

If taking on a job helps you to feel like you're doing something concrete to face your grief, consider an after-school job with few responsibilities and a light schedule. Talk to your potential employer about your reasons for wanting to work, so you're both on the same page. As a seasoned businessperson, your employer might have helpful insight into how to use your work to best process your loss.

My younger siblings are driving me nuts. Why don't they understand what I'm going through?

When our hearts and minds are already preoccupied with grief, the last thing we want is a sibling to come and annoy us. If you both lost someone in common, they might be dealing with that sadness in a way that isn't helping you.

Little kids experience grief differently than teenagers and adults do. They often pop in and out of sadness. For example, your little sister might be cheerful and running around until she trips and everything falls apart. With tears rolling down her cheeks, she might cry

PRAYER AND SCRIPTURE

God, as if it wasn't hard enough that I had to lose _____, now my whole life feels like it's changing. It's as if the world I lived in totally disappeared when they died. Help me to trust that you are with me in all of these changes. Remind me of your presence beside me when it feels like grief has shifted everything. Thank you that I can count on you to stay the same always and forever. Thank you for guiding me as I learn to live without _____. Amen.

> I waited patiently for God to help me; then he listened and heard my cry. He lifted me out of the pit of despair, out from the bog and the mire, and set my feet on a hard, firm path, and steadied me as I walked along.
> PSALM 40:1-2, TLB

> "I know what I'm doing. I have it all planned out—plans to take care of you, not abandon you, plans to give you the future you hope for."
> JEREMIAH 29:11, MSG

that she misses her person—not that her knee hurts! Your brother might seem fine all day until bedtime, when tiredness and the darkness begin to unravel his emotions. Your sibling might be so little that he or she never mentions the deceased person at all—even if it was a parent. From your position as a teenager, it can be hard to understand that these things can even be true.

If you're struggling with these relationships, go easy on yourself. Talk to a parent or other adult for relief and try to create some quiet space in your day where you can be alone with *your* emotions. In these cases, it's also helpful to remember that even though their expression of grief is different from yours, you still need to treat your siblings with love. Even when you can't see it, they carry grief too. And as they get older and begin to realize everything their loss means, they'll need you there as a wise guide and friend to help them navigate a life you've already learned to live because you're older.

If a friend of yours died or you lost someone your siblings don't know well, they might not understand why you're feeling the way you are. They may not feel any grief at all because they're not close to the situation and they haven't lost a relationship.

If you find yourself there, have a little heart-to-heart with your sibling in age-appropriate language. Explain that your loss makes you sad and that you need to make room for that sadness in your life—as if an extra person is sitting on the couch. Apologize for being short-tempered when grief makes you lose your cool. And because little kids love to help, let your sibling know what helps you most—a hug, a hand-drawn card, a back rub, or someone to snuggle up with you on your bed. You might be surprised to receive a heaping dose of compassion from a younger heart that knows what it means to need love when life feels hard.

Who do I tell about my person's death, and how do I tell them?

You can tell anyone you want about what happened. You might not want to say anything because it's awkward, but your person's death isn't something that you need to keep a secret. You can share your story when and with whom you wish when you're ready.

When you do want to tell someone about your loss, you get to say as much or as little as you want. I (Fiona) usually only mention that my dad died a few years ago. Some people say, "I'm sorry," and quickly change the subject. I've come to accept that. It's a good clue that they're not people I'll be able to share much of my story with, and I make a mental note of this. Other people ask follow-up questions like "How did he die?" or "How are you doing?" I've learned to be prepared for these responses too. Sometimes the person is just curious, but I've found that most people really do care about my loss and how it has affected me. It feels good to be able to talk about my dad and show them that I'm still a normal person just like they are.

You are the gatekeeper of your story. Just like a knight standing guard at a medieval castle, you get to decide who enters your story and who doesn't. You get to decide how much detail a person receives. You get to decide whether a person is worthy of knowing the tenderest parts of your loss. We recommend that you give some thought to who these people might be in your life—classmates, teammates, your youth pastor, or other trusted adults. The "Who Are My People?" activity on page 29 can help you discern who might be a good person to share parts of your story with.

There is one challenge to sharing your story, and we wouldn't be honest if we didn't bring it up. Sometimes sharing your story can create distance between you and the person you've told. Sometimes a friend just isn't able to receive your story or walk with you through it. In the grief community we call this a "secondary loss" because it can feel like another death, losing a living relationship on top of losing the person who died.

Unfortunately, relational risk is something we all experience. We step out in hope that a classmate will be a potential friend, only to discover that we don't really click. A friendship that we've had since we were little starts to thin as we grow older and head off to different schools. We deal with these sorts of changes all the time, but in grief the changes can feel more painful. We want you to know that this is possible. There may be some people who drift out of your life after you tell them your story.

Sharing your story might mean risking a friendship, but it might also introduce new relationships that bring unexpected life and joy. Through courageously sharing your story, you may discover that an acquaintance knows a similar kind of loss. Your shared grief could bond you to one another. You may discover that your story gives courage to someone who is facing a different kind of trial but who

WHAT DO I SAY?

Top Ten Responses to Help You When You Don't Have Words

After your person dies, people ask you so many questions! Sometimes it's hard to answer because grief feels like it's talking really loudly in your head and you can't focus. Other times, you genuinely don't have an answer. Often, it's hard to even come up with the words to say.

Here's a list of our top ten favorite responses when you don't have words. Ditch the age-old "I dunno" and try one of these when you're asked a question you're not ready or not able to answer.

1. I'm not ready to talk about that right now.
2. I'm having a hard day and need some space.
3. I'll let you know if I need help.
4. Thanks for inviting me. Maybe I can attend another time.
5. I need some time to think about that.
6. I'm not sure how to answer that question.
7. I'm not making any big decisions right now.
8. I trust I'll know when I'm ready.
9. I could always use prayer.

And perhaps our all-time favorite . . .

10. No, thank you. (Yup, it's okay to say no.)

can commit to praying with and for you as you walk through your unique hard stories side by side. Grief can break apart relationships, but it can also build new, beautiful ones. As you take the vulnerable step to share with others, remember this and take heart.

Can I just not tell anybody at all about my loss?

There will definitely be times when people mention or ask about your person, and you don't want to say anything. In these cases, it will be up to you whether to tell them what happened. If your hairstylist asks about your family, you don't need to mention that one of them has died if you don't want to. If the dentist refers to your dad and he's not here anymore, you don't necessarily need to correct her. Not everybody in your life is on intimate, "need to know" status. Sometimes it's okay to say nothing.

If you choose not to answer, be sure you're doing it for privacy reasons and not because you're hiding. While there is no obligation for you to tell someone, keeping your loss a secret won't help you move forward and grow with your grief. Secrets are rarely healthy; and, in the case of grief, secrets only serve to isolate you from potential sources of support. It is important to have people who will support you. Be sure you have at least one good friend or trusted adult you can talk to.

Everybody says, "I'm sorry for your loss." I'm sorry too! How do I respond?

We can't name one person who hasn't said that to us! It is probably the most common and least helpful thing that everyone says. Honestly, though, we don't blame them. Most people don't know how to talk about grief. Sometimes we don't either.

It's been five years since our loss, and still when someone says, "I'm sorry for your loss," we never quite know what to say. You don't say, "I forgive you," because they haven't done anything wrong. You don't say, "It's okay," because really it's not!

In our experience, "I'm sorry for your loss" is a poor modern translation of the old-fashioned statement "My condolences." When someone offers their condolences to you, they are expressing sympathy and compassion. The word *condolence* actually means "suffer together."[2] "My condolences" means you're suffering with the person over what they've lost.

Our modern rendering of "I'm sorry for your loss" doesn't set you up for success, but if you can see the "suffering together" sentiment behind it, you might find it easier to respond. When someone says those infamous words now, you don't have to feel awkward about it. You can just reply with "Thank you," knowing that this may be the best way that person knows to express that they care.

What about all the other dumb stuff they say?

Unfortunately, people will say a lot of dumb stuff. Let's run through a few of the real doozies.

"**GOD NEEDED ANOTHER ANGEL.**" Nope. This is just fluffy feel-good talk. The Bible is our ultimate authority, and there is nothing in Scripture that says we become angels when we die. In fact, Psalm 148 makes a clear distinction between angels and humans when it instructs both groups separately to praise God.[3]

"**GOD ONLY TAKES THE GOOD ONES.**" No, again. Ecclesiastes 9 reminds us, "All share a common destiny—the righteous and the wicked, the good and the bad. . . . As it is with the good, so with the sinful."[4] God doesn't take people because of how good they are. He moves in ways that we don't understand. God is not the mean guy who removes all of the M&M's from the trail mix and leaves the nuts and raisins behind. In reality, we're all bad because of our sin. Thanks be to God that because of Jesus' death and resurrection, our slates are wiped clean, and God sees us as redeemed and forgiven!

"**IT COULD BE WORSE.**" Well, maybe, but not helpful! Your home could be destroyed, you could lose all your friends, and you could be stricken with illness. The Old Testament character Job knew that all too well. His life was totally destroyed by loss. Yes, it could be worse. However, loss isn't a comparison game. You don't need to have the entire world cave in to receive compassion and kindness from those around you. In losing someone you love, in a sense, your entire world *has* caved in around you. You deserve to be noticed for this.

"TAKE HEART. THEY'RE IN HEAVEN." This is an especially tough one because, if your person loved Jesus, it's actually true. However, we put this in the "Well, maybe, but not helpful" category too. Here's why. Most of the time, this comment simply attempts to redirect our attention away from the pain of our loss. However, the apostle Paul told his friends at the church in Philippi, "I'm torn between two desires: I long to go and be with Christ, which would be far better for me. But for your sakes, it is better that I continue to live."[5] Paul understood that perfect peace is found only in God's presence, and he longed to be rid of earth's sadness and enveloped in eternal joy. He also knew that physical presence with those we love means a great deal. He wasn't so heavenly minded that he was no earthly good. Paul recognized that loving community gives us a foretaste of the joy that heaven will offer. So, yes. We're glad your person is in the presence of Jesus, seeing him face-to-face. We anticipate that reunion with joy one day too! *And* we're *also* sad that your person isn't in *your* presence, seeing *you* face-to-face. The gain of glory does not overshadow this loss.

When I try to share about my loss, the other person starts telling me their own grief story. Who is supposed to be comforting whom?

This happens a lot. You're talking about your person, and all of a sudden you're hearing a story about someone's great-great-aunt dying or their distant relative who has cancer or—worst of all—their pet dying. You've gone from trying to share your story and receive comfort to wondering whether you should be offering your condolences instead! To make it worse, none of these stories actually makes

IN THEIR OWN WORDS: VIOLET'S STORY

My dad died unexpectedly of leukemia two years ago. In the days that immediately followed, I felt nothing. I had convinced myself that it was all a dream and that he was going to come back. A couple months later, I finally had a grasp on the fact that I was never going to hug him again, and he was never going to pick us up from school again.

At the beginning of the next school year, I tried the sports that I once enjoyed playing while my dad cheered me on, but I couldn't do it. Lacrosse goals meant nothing if he wasn't the loudest person yelling for me. Cross-country races weren't worth finishing if he wasn't there waiting to tell me I did a great job. I detached myself from everything and relied on music. Never taking my headphones out, I blasted music that we listened to together and music that was just as down as I was.

After a long season of depression, anxiety, and many other bad things, I started to rely on God. I went to church, took notes, and talked to my mom about it. I surrounded myself with people who loved the Lord as much as I strove to. God gave me peace, joy, and confidence, and he took my scars away.

—Violet, age 15, whose dad died two years prior

you feel better because they're nothing like the sadness you're living through right now.

Our brains have these amazing things called mirror neurons. They help us to read the emotions of other people. When you're sad, the mirror neurons in my brain help me notice your facial expressions and miraculously, without realizing it, I mirror those expressions back to you. That's why it feels totally wrong to laugh in the face of someone who is crying. It goes against everything our brains tell us to do.

When we're trying to relate to other people, we often do a similar thing. We look for common connections and try to accentuate them. Do you like the Red Sox? *Me too!* You're worried about the history test next week? *Me too!* As if looking in a mirror, we search for stuff that is familiar to orient and connect ourselves to those around us.

I suspect that the person you've talked to wanted to do just that. He or she wanted to say, "I understand," and began sharing a story to try to find common ground. In one respect, your friend is right—loss is loss is loss. We don't need to share all the exact same details to find strength and comfort from one another's stories.

However, there's a right time and place to share a grief story, and when you're trying to share yours, it can feel disrespectful, confusing, or even offensive to have someone else share a story that doesn't seem to match the grief you're facing. If you desire to share your story with someone, you probably don't want to acknowledge the common human experience of loss. Instead, you want to sit with the unique sadness that has come into your life through the death of a particular person. If this is the case, simply thank the person for their story and move on. You don't need to offer comfort.

My friends stopped texting me and wanting to get together. Why? I'm so lonely now.

Our hearts break to know that you're feeling alone as you cope with your loss. Nobody should have to go through grief alone. Whether your friends are just trying to give you some space or they don't know what to do, it hurts to feel like you've been abandoned in your greatest moment of need. You may never actually know what has brought on their radio silence.

First, we want you to know that Jesus understands. After inviting his friends to the garden of Gethsemane to wait and pray, Jesus turned around to discover that they'd all fallen asleep. It was as though nobody could read the room and see that Jesus was anxious and afraid. He'd even *told* them he was troubled![6] When Jesus most needed someone to encourage, support, and befriend him, he found himself all alone. He understands your loneliness, and his heart aches for you too.

Second, we encourage you to let your friends know that you miss them. Tell them how much you value their presence in your life. Remind them that they are important to you! After you've done this, work to enhance the relationships you have before you. Focus on the people you see every day—your family, your teammates, the person who sits next to you in English class. Put down your phone so that you don't obsessively check for texts and engage as you're able with the people you have right in front of you. While this won't necessarily take away the loneliness of your friends' quiet season, it can turn this time into a comfort to you. We can always use more relationships in our lives, and this season may offer you an opportunity to build new friendships.

My parents want me to go to a support group. Will I like it?

While every support group is different, we definitely see the value in spending time with other people who have experienced losses like you have. Will it be awkward at first? Yes, probably. However, as time goes by, you'll get to know the other students in your group. You'll learn that it's safe to share, and you may even learn some new tools and tricks to help you navigate your life with grief better.

After our loss, our family went to a family support group together for a special evening activity. Before breaking into family units to make our craft, we sat in a big circle in the attic of the support center. One by one, we introduced ourselves around the circle, a circle that was bigger than we'd expected when we signed up. Each family shared their names and the person they'd lost. Everyone had experienced the death of a parent.

At first, it was awkward to think about introducing ourselves, but after a few people started, it became clear: we were in a room of people *just like us.* For the first (and perhaps only) time, in this setting our family wasn't weird for living with grief. We were normal, just like everyone else.

This normalcy is one of the gifts of a support group. At school or church or work, you may be the only person who lives with your particular loss. In a support group, though, loss *is* the norm. The comfort of being known just as you are can give you the courage to participate fully and really grow from the experience. We encourage you to try it!

My relatives keep asking how I'm doing, and it bugs me. How do I get them to stop?

One thing my mom taught us after my dad died was to stand up for ourselves. If someone asked a question we didn't feel comfortable answering or put us in an awkward situation, we could say no.

When you are grieving, you are in charge. This can be a real relief when it feels like everything else in your life has spun out of control. Your relatives might be going through their own process of grief, but you don't have to answer their questions or have a conversation with them about your loss if you don't want to. You are free to say, "I don't want to talk about that," or excuse yourself to a different room.

Standing up for yourself is important to upholding the boundaries that you need while you are grieving. You can choose who you invite into your grief experience and who remains outside that circle of trust. For any number of reasons, your relatives might not be good or healthy people to invite into that circle. That's 100 percent okay. Celebrate those family members with whom you can be honest, and politely change the subject with those you can't.

3

ALL THE FEELS

One of my (Clarissa's) favorite Pixar movies is *Inside Out*. In it, we get a sneak peek into the emotions that swirl around in a young girl's head. As Riley adjusts to her family's move to San Francisco, we meet all the internal "characters" who come along with her—Joy, Sadness, Anger, Disgust, and Fear. In one scene, Joy and Sadness wander together, lost at the edge of Long-Term Memory. Sadness lies down on the ground and laments, "I'm too sad to walk. Just give me a few . . . hours."[1] Unwilling to stand around and wait, Joy grabs her leg and drags her onward. I don't know about you, but I've felt like Sadness more than once.

We talked about our bodies (chapter 1) and the practical elements of our loss (chapter 2) first because addressing these dimensions of our grief helps to create a healthy foundation to face the ongoing emotions that come with the death of a loved one.

Unfortunately, though, we can't do one and then the other.

Most likely, you'll have to take care of practical things like school and friendships *at the same time* as you take care of your emotions. You won't get a time-out to rest your body before you have to deal with your sadness. However, here's what we have found. In the words of therapist Dr. Jenn Hardy, "The routines you are able to maintain during a crisis are the ropes you will use to pull yourself through, back to yourself."[2] The habits and actions we've talked about so far will help to make your life easier as you focus on the big, long-term work with those "internal characters" in your own head and heart.

When we think about the feelings that come with loss, it helps to remember that sadness is only one of them. Relationships are complex, and so are you! Your relationship with the person you lost will reveal particular emotions. Your relationships with those left behind—your friends and family, even strangers—will reveal other emotions. Like Riley in *Inside Out*, you'll have lots of voices in your head wanting to be heard. The most important thing to remember as you face these big feelings is this: every single voice belongs.

Imagine for a moment that those characters in *Inside Out* are sitting in a classroom at your school. Joy sits in the front row; she's just that kind of girl. Disgust and Fear take the back seats against the wall. Anger parks himself in the middle of the classroom, where he'll be easily noticed. Sadness slumps into the seat closest to the door; she doesn't even want to be here.

In every classroom, there are students who like to answer questions and those who hold back. There are students who like to draw attention to themselves and those who'd like to disappear into the woodwork. Whether or not a student wants to raise a hand in class, each body in each seat matters.

The same is true for your emotions. In the classroom of your heart, you're the teacher. You stand at the front and get to choose who speaks. Does Fear often raise her hand to share? You need to listen to her. Do you sense Anger has something to say but doesn't feel brave enough to say it? Maybe it's time to create space in your day to let Anger speak. Does Sadness seem to want to drown out all the other emotions? It's okay to ask her to be quiet for a moment so Joy can finally talk. All your emotions—both the loud and the quiet voices—have important things to say about your loss.

If your loss was sudden, you may feel a strong sense of shock and numbness. As your brain tries to wrap itself around the reality of death, you may not be sure what to feel. Other times, you may experience a jumble of emotions: laughing and crying within the same day or hour, or even at the same time. One overriding emotion—fear, for example, or anger—may seem to color everything. If your loss occurred because of a crime, you may feel a strong sense of righteous anger. If your loss occurred because of suicide, you may feel betrayal or confusion. All these emotions are like students in your heart's classroom that are clamoring to speak.

HE CALLS THEM GOOD

When God knit you together in your mother's womb, he made your eyes and your fingers and toes. He also made your capacity for emotion. Like all of the things God made, God called this capacity "good."[3] Earthworms, humpback whales, and chimpanzees display God's wonderful design and creativity, but only you reflect the vast diversity of God's own emotional character. In your body and in your wiring, you carry within you the *imago dei*, the image of God.

At Creation, God said, "Let us make human beings in our image, to be like us."[4] What an incredible honor! Like a mirror we reflect back to God and to the world around us what God is like. We love because God loves. We create because God creates. And, yes, we grieve because God grieves. Our capacity to feel deeply is a gift from God.

QUIZ: INTUITIVE AND INSTRUMENTAL GRIEVING

Kenneth Doka and Terry Martin researched grieving people and learned that not all people grieve the same way. More than that, they discovered that grief isn't something that males do one way and females do another way.[5] Instead, each person grieves in a way that fits their personality.

Doka and Martin called people who need to emotionally express their grief "intuitive" grievers. These people experience big feelings and feel comfortable letting them out either on their own or with others. They called people who feel an urge to *do* something with their grief "instrumental" grievers. Rather than crying a lot, you'll probably find these people learning about the health condition that took their person's life, starting a nonprofit in their memory, or sorting through their belongings to decide what to keep and what to give away.

Most people aren't all intuitive or all instrumental; more often, we are a mix of the two. Circle the numbers of the statements below that most accurately describe how you feel about your loss. Tally up your responses and see what grieving process comes most naturally to you.

1. I feel a lot better after I've had a good cry.
2. I don't often show it on the outside, but I'm really sad that my person died.

More than that, it is a gift that ties us inextricably to him. As we experience the emotional range and capacity that he gave us, we have the opportunity to let that experience connect us more intimately to him.

You may have been taught that some emotions are good and some are bad. For example, anger, fear, or frustration are bad, while calm, happiness, and excitement are good. As you learn to live with your grief, I encourage you to release these good/bad categories. Emotions in and of themselves aren't right or wrong. Instead, they're messengers. They carry important words to our hearts and heads about the past, the present, and the future. They articulate a perspective about

3. I really want to talk about my person with other people.
4. I think about my person a lot when I'm doing other things.
5. Looking at pictures of my person makes me cry, but I like to do it anyway.
6. I want to understand the details of my person's death.
7. Sometimes I talk to my person, even though I know they're dead.
8. I feel a lot better after I've taken a run or played a hard game of basketball.
9. When I feel angry, I just want to yell.
10. My person's death has made me want to make some big changes in my life.

IF YOU CIRCLED MOSTLY ODD-NUMBERED RESPONSES, you've got a strong urge to express your grief in intuitive ways. Journaling, talking with a friend, or even crying alone can offer you relief from grief's hardest emotions. You acknowledge your pain by letting it show, and that's a really healthy thing to do!

IF YOU CIRCLED MOSTLY EVEN-NUMBERED RESPONSES, instrumental grieving is the way you feel most yourself. You can hit balls at the batting cage, participate in a fundraiser for a cause in memory of your person, or challenge yourself to imitate your loved one's better qualities. You're a doer, and your emotions feel most released when you've got a plan for your body, your mind, and your time. Your willingness to meet grief face-to-face is already making you a resilient person.

the situations we face and what we've been through. Are our emotions always accurate descriptions of what's going on in the world? No. Nevertheless, they're still important. Our emotions disclose the inner workings of our hearts, and they reveal to us the spaces we need Jesus to fill. Your emotions are all good—very good. It's what you do with them that matters most.

When Jesus got sad, he didn't bottle it up. He wept.[6] When Jesus got angry, he didn't explode in expletives. He executed justice by ridding the Temple of thieving merchants.[7] When Jesus was despairing, he didn't put on a tough front. He asked his friends to stay near and support him.[8] Jesus, the perfect *imago dei*, "the image of the invisible God," showed us how to listen to and live with our emotions.[9] Jesus showed us how to feel all the feels and survive by clinging to our heavenly Father.

Jesus cares whether you're getting enough sleep since your person's death. He cares about that vacation you had to miss because of the funeral. And because he is deeply acquainted with suffering, Jesus cares about the emotions that lobby for attention in your head and heart. Let's consider some specifics about those feelings to help you navigate this important dimension of your life with grief.

YOUR QUESTIONS ANSWERED

To cry or not to cry? That is the question.

Full disclosure: I (Clarissa) cry a lot. This doesn't embarrass Fiona (thank goodness!), but it definitely embarrasses her brother. He's not much of a crier; it's just not how he's wired. I've cried a lot in the last five years—in the grocery store, at church, in the car, at school events, and even at work. Something reminds me of my loss, and the waterworks turn on. Staring at the ceiling and thinking funny thoughts rarely helps. If I'm going to cry, I just have to let the tears empty themselves.

The loss of your person can make crying feel like a big deal. Will you cry at the funeral? If you don't cry often, does that mean you don't miss your person? What if you don't want to cry in front of certain people? Is it okay to cry alone? Some people who used to wear their hearts on their sleeves find their tears dry up after loss. Others who were previously pretty stoic find they melt into a puddle at the name of the person who died.

Science tells us a few important things about crying. Crying helps to regulate our breathing. It wears us out, and it lowers our blood pressure. There are clear benefits to having a good cry every once in a while. Our bodies appreciate the release, and tears can bring us to exhaustion, which prompts sleep and rest to return us to equilibrium. A person who bottles up their emotions will find that those emotions come out in other ways, not always healthy or good ones.

As you learn to live with your grief, know that whatever feels right for you is just fine when it comes to crying. If it feels natural to shed a tear, go ahead and do it without embarrassment. Humans cry when they are hurt. If tears well up in your eyes, it's okay to let them fall. There's no such thing as "Big girls don't cry" or "Real men don't cry."

If tears don't feel natural to you, that's okay too. Check in with your heart to make sure you're finding healthy outlets for your feelings—through self-expression like journaling, music, or art, or in conversations with trusted friends. Then experience the freedom to move on from the discussion. If tears are to come, they'll come when they're ready.

How do I handle my emotions when I'm at school, work, or church?

Emotions don't take note of our location. They show up when and where they want to. This can be really difficult when you're learning to live with grief. Like a little kid melting down in the aisle at Target, your grief might decide to show up in a public place; and its outburst might be startling or embarrassing. What do you do when grief decides to speak when you're out and about? You're going to want to treat it like that poor, sweet kid in the store.

We've all seen it before, the parent who scolds a child in the middle of the aisle because she's crying that she can't have candy. Public shaming or discipline rarely works in these situations, and it doesn't work well for grief either. Most often, a lecture about appropriate behavior in public just leads to more tears of frustration. We feel what we feel when we feel it. Plus, often those feelings are very big and very, very real. When grief shows up, it needs an outlet.

As you recognize grief bubbling up at school, work, or church, do what many parents have found to work best in the aisle of Target. Dismiss yourself from the location to give your grief some space. Ask to go to the bathroom. Step out into the hallway. Get permission to stop by your school counselor's office. Close your eyes and take a deep breath to still your body and mind. If possible, let your grief moment run its course, and regain composure.

You are welcome in all places with all your emotions, and you don't need to shut down to cope. Instead, like the parent with the crying child, you can "leave your cart in the aisle," step outside, and let the moment wash over you. Then, when you're ready, you can return to what you were doing. Class will still be going; you can get the missed notes from a friend. Work will cover for you at the cash register just as they would if you needed a bathroom break. Church will welcome you in whatever condition you're in, puffy eyes and all. A follow-up conversation with your teacher or work supervisor will alert them to your needs. That way, if and when you need space again, you'll have an adult nearby who understands why life feels hard and can accommodate and support you.

Sometimes I feel guilty about how angry I am. What should I do?

You may not have anticipated it, but anger is a normal emotion to experience after the death of a loved one. It's normal to be angry at health professionals who missed a diagnosis or couldn't save a life. It's natural to be angry at your family or your friends or the world in general that doesn't seem to understand how you're feeling. It's okay to be angry with God and filled with questions about the tragedy that has entered your life. It's even okay to be angry with your dead person—for dying, for leaving a conflict unresolved, for not being the person you needed him or her to be, for anything at all.

Now that we know it's okay to be angry, what do we do with this emotion? Thankfully the Bible gives us lots of guidance on how to handle our anger. (The Bible tells us that God gets angry sometimes, especially at sin [see Psalm 78:21-22], so he knows we need help!)

In our anger, we need to be careful of falling into sin. "Be angry and do not sin; do not let the sun go down on your anger," Paul says to the Ephesian church.[10] Anger can give birth to meanness, jealousy, gossip, scornful speech, and hatred. It can cause deep rifts between you and your parents that take a long time to heal. As you experience anger, remember that it's a lot like poison ivy. It grows quickly and can easily take over everything.

Because of this, it's a good idea to regularly bring your anger to God. When Paul tells the church not to let the sun go down on their anger, he's encouraging them to keep daily short accounts. Instead of stewing about something, make things right with your parent before you go to bed. Don't wait. Talk to God about your angry feelings and ask him to help you release them.

Psalm 7 tells us that "God is a righteous judge, and a God who feels indignation every day."[11] If you're worried that your anger is weird or unusual, take heart. It's a familiar emotion for your heavenly Father. Here's the true comfort, though: not only does God experience anger with the brokenness of the world, but he's the one who has the power to fix it. Both frustrated with sin, death, and the devil *and* capable of righteous judgment, God stands where we cannot. He alone can right the wrongs that frustrate and anger us; he's the only one who can repair this heartsick, sorrowful world.

As you witness your anger with self-compassion and avoid sinfulness, as you bring your anger to God, look for the emotion that might be lurking behind your anger. Often, sadness or fear is trying to speak but doesn't quite know how. You may find it helpful to share your feelings with a trusted adult who can help you identify the driving emotion behind anger. Once you know what's really bugging you, you can more easily address it.

THE WHEEL OF EMOTIONS

You may have seen Robert Plutchik's wheel of emotions hanging on your classroom wall when you were a little kid. Sometimes younger kids have trouble putting words to their emotions, and a drawing can be really helpful. The emotions wheel isn't just for little kids, though! *All people* have trouble putting words to their emotions sometimes.

If you've been asked how you're doing lately and you responded with a bland "Fine," you might benefit from a spin or two of the emotions wheel. Robert Plutchik designed it brilliantly with intense emotions toward the center and less intense ones on the outer ring. Are you feeling terrified about something related to your loss? Or would *fear* or *apprehension* be a better way to describe your feelings? Thanks to the wheel of emotions, you've got an expanded vocabulary to identify and talk about that crazy swirl of stuff going around in your head and heart.

How to Make the Wheel of Emotions Work for You

Are you feeling a very intense emotion right now? Trace your finger on the petal of the wheel to discover the outermost emotion associated with it. What might you need to move from rage to simple annoyance? A long walk with a friend? Some time away from the comparison of social media? A good night's sleep? It can work the other direction too. Are you feeling blah and want to experience more joy in your life? What might you need to do to move from the outer ring of emotions to a more satisfying feeling?

When you're able to identify your emotions, you can sit with them like you would with a friend, listening to their needs and figuring out how to care for yourself in the midst of your feelings. You can recognize your emotions not as wrong or right but simply as indicators of your heart's condition at the moment. You can take your heart's temperature by checking in on your emotions.

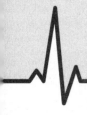

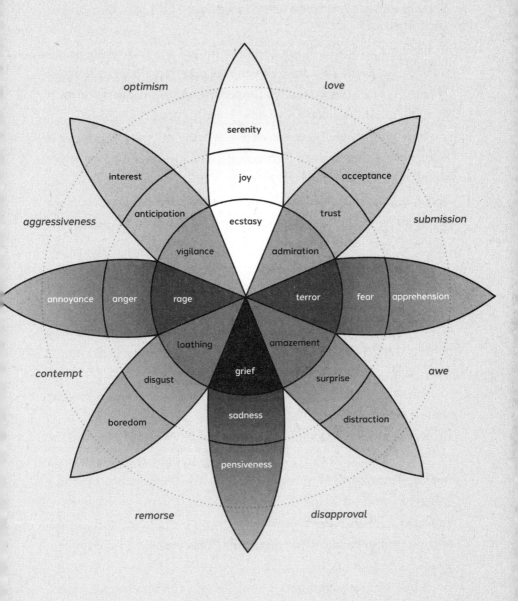

People expect me to be emotional, but I just feel numb. Is that normal?

It might surprise you to learn that numbness is a very normal reaction to the death of a loved one. You may experience numbness because of shock, especially if your person's death surprised you with its suddenness, its violence, or how it was communicated.

Your sympathetic nervous system is what prompts you to fight or flight, but that's not all it does. Sometimes it causes you to freeze. Think for a moment how this capacity might actually be a mercy. You hear a bee buzzing near your ear, and instead of running away from the sound you get the instinct to hold very still until the bee gets bored and flies away. Freezing has protected you from being stung.

In a similar—but much bigger—way, the freeze capacity of your nervous system offers you mercy in the face of grief's acute pain. As your brain begins to take in all the details of your loss, you experience a numbness that freezes you so that your whole body can begin to process the depth and breadth of what it will mean to live without your person.

Will the numbness wear off? Yes, at some point it will. Like your mouth after you've received a shot of Novocain at the dentist, your life will feel weird for a while, and other emotions might seem distant or inaccessible. Little by little, though, as your brain processes all that has happened, you'll begin to feel again. You'll experience new and different emotions, some of them more intense than you might have expected. The hurt might hurt worse as you begin to feel fully again, and numbness might seem preferable. That's where what happens next is so important.

While feeling numb about your loss is normal, especially soon after your person's death, it isn't healthy to stay that way forever. Your sympathetic nervous system was designed for intermittent functioning, not heavy everyday use, and when it experiences repeated overwhelm, a different kind of numbness can set in that looks a lot like despair. That's why it's super important, as you emerge from numbness, to engage the other amazing part of your nervous system—the parasympathetic side, a system committed to restoration.

In a life where it feels like a lot has happened to you that you can't control, you can control this. You get to decide whether the numbness is only a single step on the pathway to greater emotional depth or it becomes an addiction to avoid pain. You can choose to reconnect with those you love, engage in hobbies or activities that fuel your passions, and worship, rest, and pray to commune deeply with God. You can be an active participant in your restoration.

If you've gone back to your regular routines and a lot of time has passed and you *still* feel numb, we recommend talking to a counselor who can help you regulate your nervous system and move toward health and well-being. It may take a long time for you to find joy in life post-loss, but it's possible.

I'm tired of big feelings. When will I feel like myself again?

Because of your loss, you're a person who now understands a part of the world you didn't before. That reality is literally life-changing. You can't step back into a black-and-white world now that you've seen the world's full colors. You know too much now to do that convincingly.

If you can't get back to the person you were before, you've got two choices: you can lament the *you* you've lost, or you can meet the *you* you are now. We actually recommend you do both. First, take the time to lament the you you've lost in your person's death. Did you have to grow up fast? Do you notice sadness where you didn't before? Go ahead and grieve those changes. They're big and real, and they hurt. Grieve them whenever you notice the disconnect between who you are now and who you used to be. Tell God you miss the old you. Tell him that it's painful to feel like you don't even know yourself anymore.

While you stay honest about what you've lost, we encourage you to find ways to "meet" the you who you are now. Do you reach out with compassion to others more readily now because of the loss you've experienced in your own life? Are you more thoughtful about how you spend your time? Can you find pleasure in simple things that you may have overlooked before? What gifts has grief unexpectedly brought into your life to change you into who you are today?

The apostle Peter describes suffering as passing through a refining fire.[12] The painful circumstances we encounter in life offer us opportunities to be shaped and changed. For you, the death of your person offers one such opportunity. If you can't turn back the clock and be who you were before, who might you like to be *now*? How can what's happened in your life shape you into a person who looks more like Jesus? As you meet the new you, you'll inevitably find that some things have stayed the same—you still love rocky road ice cream or a challenging pickup game of basketball. You'll also find that some things have changed. As you walk close to Jesus, you'll find that the new you, refined by the fire of suffering, is a beautiful thing to behold.

My parents asked if I'm depressed. Am I?

We want you to take good care of your mental health as you walk with grief and begin your new life without your person. While they can look a lot alike, grief and depression are actually two different things. One is the natural response to loss; the other is an ongoing struggle with difficult thoughts. Your parents sound concerned about you, and an honest conversation with them might be a good place to start.

First, find out where your parents have concerns. Do they notice changes you haven't—in your social relationships, in your diet, or in your sleep patterns? Keep an open mind as you hear their feedback, remembering that we can't always see ourselves clearly. Sometimes we need someone to let us know we've got a smear of food on our face. Listen without arguing; receive their concerns as wholehearted love, not criticism.

Once you understand your parents' concerns, share with them your real feelings. Are there things you haven't told them that would help to explain your behavior? Your honesty can build a bridge to understanding and help you and your parents assess *together* what is best for you. As you share, be sure to view yourself with self-compassion. Nobody gets in trouble for grieving. We suspect your parents simply want you to walk with grief in a way that's healthy. You may have to learn together what that looks like for you.

Finally, determine together whether talking to another supportive person might be a good idea. A trauma-informed therapist or a grief counselor might be a helpful resource as you figure out whether your feelings and behaviors are typical for grief or if you need additional mental health care. The great thing about professionals is that they've seen *lots* of other people like you before. Nothing you say or do will surprise them. They're excellent noticers and are trained to care for you.

Will another terrible thing happen? Do bad things really come in threes?

Bad things do not come in threes. They come by themselves, in bunches, and sometimes hardly ever. That is to say, you can't predict disaster. After we encounter death, our worries can make us almost superstitious. We double-check the front door lock before going to bed, or we sleep with our phones, or we stop doing activities we once enjoyed because we wonder if changing our lives could actually prevent something else bad from happening.

Unfortunately, life happens, and we have very little control over it. Behind all of our fears and superstitious behaviors is that terrifying reality. Bad things happen, and we can't always stop them. If your person's death is the first terrible thing that's ever happened in your life, this reality can totally disarm you. You thought you were

WHEN YOU NEED MORE HELP

The famous actress Lily Collins once said, "Asking for help is never a sign of weakness. It's one of the bravest things you can do. And it can save your life."[13] We agree 100 percent. Even as you learn to face and accept the feelings of your grief, you may find that you still are feeling overwhelmed, anxious, or despairing. If you do, the bravest action you can take is to ask for help.

Suicidal thoughts, anxiety, and depression aren't sinful. Instead, they're signals. They're important messages that your body and your soul need care. Like a baby who wants to be held, your body, mind, and spirit cry out for attention, comfort, and peace. The brave person will always listen and respond to these messages.

If you have thoughts about hurting yourself or others, if you find your thoughts swirling in anxious worry or hopelessness, reach out to a trusted adult for help. Ask a friend to visit your school counselor with you. Talk to a parent, a coach, or a teacher. Meet with your youth pastor to let him or her know you're struggling.

As you proactively seek out help, don't give up. If there's anything that loss teaches us about the world, it's that life is incredibly precious. *Your life* is incredibly precious. With the right care and support, these feelings can lessen, and life can become more manageable.

Turn to the appendix on page 123 for numbers you can call or text that provide 24-7 care and support for mental health struggles and crises.

in control of your life before; now you wonder if anybody's even driving the bus!

I've (Clarissa) always appreciated that when Jesus decided how he'd describe himself for his people, he chose the image of a shepherd. Not a cowboy wrangling unruly cattle. Not a handler with dogs on a leash. Jesus called himself a shepherd whose job it was to guide and comfort frightened sheep.[14]

Sheep dislike being alone, and they hate loud noises, sudden movements, anything new, and—get this—places they haven't been before.[15] Basically, they're scared of everything! When a sheep leaves the fold each morning for pasture, you can be pretty well assured that it's thinking what you are: *Is another bad thing going to happen?*

When Jesus calls us his sheep and names himself as our Shepherd, he's doing more than simply saying he's in charge and we need to follow. By choosing this image, Jesus is telling us that he understands our fears. He knows that our past hurts make us nervous about future ones. He sees that what is new or unknown looks threatening because of our grief. He gets that life—even our own—feels really fragile. Jesus is our Shepherd because he knows that however many terrible things may happen, we need a strong and faithful guide to walk with us through them. We need a comforting protector to carry us when we're weak.

Your fears are natural. You've seen that this world delivers pain as well as pleasure. You know more than you used to know. Thankfully, Jesus has seen it all too. Jesus says to you, "Do not fear, for I am with you; do not be dismayed, for I am your God. I will strengthen you and help you; I will uphold you with my righteous right hand."[16] We know you'll have to return to this truth over and over again as your worries and fears pop up, but keep coming back to that familiar Shepherd's voice. He's speaking the truth.

I'm afraid that I will die—or that someone else I love will die. What should I do?

We're so sorry you're worried that you or someone else you love will die. One death is too much, and the thought of more loss must be really hard. Even though we know that one death doesn't make another happen, loss can do funny things to our logic and convince us otherwise. We worry that a funny pain in our body means we have a terminal illness. We panic when a friend doesn't call us back, worried that he's gotten into a car accident and died.

When my (Clarissa's) mind starts swirling with thoughts like these, here's a little exercise I find helpful. I call it "Concern or

Catastrophe?" A feeling of concern is rooted in facts. A feeling of catastrophe is a fact wrapped up with anxiety. When I encounter a fearful thought about someone else I love dying, my first question to myself is *Is this a concern or catastrophe?* Should the facts of the situation lead me toward genuine concern, or are the facts being obscured or overemphasized by worry? As I ask these questions of my fears, I can usually find the answer on my own. When I can't, I ask a friend outside of the situation to help me discern clearly.

Even as you work through this process, you might still be afraid of death showing up again. This is normal not only because of what has happened in your life but because death's existence in the world is real. It ultimately can't be avoided. If you find that you're struggling with constant thoughts about death, beware of the kind of media you're taking in—news, social media, or music. Steer away from content that focuses too much on death.

Death's existence means the threat of loss will always be there in one way or another. Thankfully, we can trust that God's given us a good thinking brain to determine when the threat is real and when it's not.

I laughed with some friends and then felt bad about it. Is it okay to have a good time?

After your person dies, you pretty quickly learn that there are culturally acceptable (and unacceptable) public displays of emotion. You're welcome to cry at the funeral, but a smile makes you look callous and uncaring. You can turn down invitations to sleepovers, and your friends understand. Go out for a Friday night movie? People worry that you're trying to ignore your grief. As uncomfortable as our culture might be around the sad feelings associated with loss, they're equally uncomfortable with the happy ones. What's a person to do?

We want to assure you that it is 100 percent okay for you to laugh and have a good time after your person's death. You're not callous, unfeeling, or avoidant. You're *human*! You've got a full array of emotions, and you deserve to enjoy every one. It's okay to have a good time, and no, you don't need to feel guilty about laughing.

We've talked about avoidance enough already for you to know whether your pleasure is a way of numbing yourself. We don't think you're in danger of confusing that with true happiness. However, we *are* afraid that you'll miss out on the true joys of being a teenager.

As a teenager, your grief looks a lot like adult grief. You can understand the complexities of loss. You see a future without your person. You notice regular reminders of your loved one's absence. However, because the teenage years are a time of transition, you can expect that your grief experience will also bear similarities to younger kids' bereavement experiences. That is to say, sometimes you may not think about your loss at all.

You can and should expect that you'll have moments where you live with grief like a little kid. You may find yourself absorbed with friends at school, and your loss doesn't even cross your mind. Your busy schedule of sports and after-school activities may leave you little time to ponder a future without your person. Grief may pop in and out of your life, mixing itself with laughter and really good times. None of this needs to make you feel guilty. You're just living with grief the way that's right for you.

Grief researchers tell us that this back-and-forth between loss-focused and life-focused activities is really good for a grieving brain. In fact, it's not just important for little kids; teens and adults need it too! Researchers call this pattern "oscillation," like an oscillating fan.[17] This back-and-forth movement allows grief's strength to dissipate in your life. You grow as you experience your loss *and* as you enjoy the life you still have. You develop resilience as you lean into the hard feelings *and* as you step forward to seek the joy that your future inevitably holds.

If you've wanted to laugh since your person died, go ahead and do it. And take a smiling selfie along with your laugh. Document that living with grief also means experiencing the inbreaking of joy.

Sometimes I feel guilty about arguments we had. What do I do about the stuff that can't be fixed now?

No loss is simple. Whether your person was loving or indifferent or abusive, their death brings forth all the complicated emotions that came along with that relationship while they were alive. The big difference now is that what's done is done; there's no chance for a do-over. You can't turn back time, apologize, or make amends. You can't hash out a conflict or try to work through differences.

While you can't literally talk to your person to fix the past, grief counselors agree that working through the complicated emotions associated with your loss can bring relief and resolution that allow you to move forward. Even if your person has died, you need to be able to say the things that need to be said. In fact, your person's death may be the catalyst to healing in your side of that relationship.

When you begin to feel guilty about arguments you had with your person or other problems that can't be fixed directly with your loved one, we encourage you to try these steps. You may have to do this over and over again as new emotions arise, but we've found the process helpful in offering kindness and self-compassion, as well as release from the burden of difficult memories.

1. When a hard feeling arises, **TALK TO GOD FIRST.** If necessary, confess your sin. Admit your shortcomings or identify the hurt your person did to you that was never resolved. Let God know that you need his supernatural presence to heal what has been broken. Your person isn't here, and you can't do it on your own. Reconciliation requires God's power, and through prayer you're tapping into that mercy and justice and loving-kindness.

2. **SAY OUT LOUD WHAT NEEDS TO BE SAID.** *I'm sorry. You hurt me. Please forgive me.* Whatever words you wish you could say to your person, declare them, as author Emily P. Freeman says, "with your out loud voice."[18] It might not seem like it at the moment, but there's a lot of power in simply saying out loud what's been swirling around in your head. Can your deceased loved one hear you? The Bible doesn't tell us. However, we do know that ideas crystallize, emotions release, and hope is born when we use our voices to advocate for ourselves, apologize, or seek connection.

3. **WRITE IT DOWN.** Satan loves to use the guilt we experience even after our sins are forgiven. It brings him pleasure to dig up our old junk and drag it out for display in our lives. He enjoys reminding us of wrongs done to us or ways we sinned against others. Especially when you can't be reminded of reconciliation by the physical presence of your person, Satan may take advantage of this vulnerability by causing you to forget God's mercy and kindness in your life. That's why we recommend writing your words down after you've said them out loud. Keep a reminder somewhere of the resolution you've sought, of the apology you've made. On your paper, include Psalm 103:12: "He has removed our sins as far from us as the east is from the west" (NLT). When you need reassurance that your sins (or the sins of your loved one) are covered, go back to that piece of paper. You'll have God's Word present and ready to defend you when your doubts loom large.

My life was so much better before my person died. Is it okay that I wish I was still living that life?

It's totally fine to feel that way. Right now, your life might seem pretty terrible. Death really makes a mess, whether your life was awesome before or simply good enough. In the face of loss, nothing

PRAYER AND SCRIPTURE

Jesus, you cried at your friend Lazarus's tomb. You know how it feels to be worn out from sadness. You became angry when you saw people misusing the Temple as a shopping mall. You know how it feels to be frustrated about how messed up life can be. You prayed for your own suffering to be taken away in the garden of Gethsemane. You know how it feels to want your whole life to be different.

Today, Jesus, I wish things were different. I wish all the sadness and brokenness were wiped away from the world. I wish death didn't exist. I know you've promised to come back and make all of that happen. Come quickly to make the world right again, and comfort, strengthen, and encourage me as I wait for you to fulfill your promises. Amen.

> How long, LORD? Will you forget me forever?
>   How long will you hide your face from me?
> How long must I wrestle with my thoughts
>   and day after day have sorrow in my heart?
>   How long will my enemy triumph over me?
>
> Look on me and answer, LORD my God.
>   Give light to my eyes, or I will sleep in death,
> and my enemy will say, "I have overcome him,"
>   and my foes will rejoice when I fall.
>
> But I trust in your unfailing love;
>   my heart rejoices in your salvation.
> I will sing the LORD's praise,
>   for he has been good to me.

PSALM 13

seems better than your old life. We get it. Oftentimes we feel the same way. We wish that we still lived in our old house and that our life was the way it used to be.

In the book of Genesis, a boy named Joseph was sold into slavery by his older brothers, who were jealous of him. Joseph lived in Egypt for a long time, and we're sure he missed his old life and would have given anything to be able to see his family again. For a while, life went decently for Joseph even though he lived as an exile. Eventually, though, things got bad. He was framed for assault, sent to prison, and left to languish in a cell with other men condemned to die. Nothing had turned out as he'd hoped.

Nevertheless, God hadn't forgotten Joseph. In fact, he had plans in mind that Joseph couldn't even imagine. Years later, when Joseph saw his brothers again, he told them, "You intended to harm me, but God intended it for good."[19] God had good plans for Joseph even through the horrible things that had happened to him. There was no "better life" Joseph had lived before his tragedy. All of it—the good and the bad—was part of the beautiful tapestry God was weaving.

Every time I (Fiona) think that my life was so much better before my dad died and I wish that I could go back, I try to remember that God has great things in store for me both now and in the future. The past isn't the only place where God blessed me. If I have eyes to see, I'll notice that he's caring for me now and charting out a course for me that will bring me joy as I follow him.

It is totally normal to wish you had your old life back—that's a natural part of grieving and saying goodbye. As you experience these feelings, keep in mind that God is going to use the hard things you've gone through to grow you into the person he made you to be. You can hold the longing for your old life and your hope for tomorrow in the same hand as you walk with grief today. From the time he formed you in your mom's womb, God has had good plans for your life.[20] Even in the mystery of grief, he's working on those plans right now.

What do I say online about my person's death?

For better or worse, social media has become the place where we're used to sharing our feelings. We record funny TikTok videos to make our friends laugh, and we post Instagram tributes for people we've lost. Whether we feel a sense of anonymity because we can say things without actually looking someone in the eye, or we find it's helpful to get information to a lot of people at once, social media allows us to talk about our loss in ways we might not otherwise. Which can be good . . . and bad.

We all need to get used to talking about our loss with people we trust. Grief isn't something we need to hide. Sometimes an online grief community can be an incredible blessing—a gathering of people who know what loss feels like. If you're struggling, an online support group can be a great source of comfort.

But grief is also something sacred. Not everybody deserves to have a window into your soul. You may find that posting on social media about your loved one invites others to care for you or to speak words of encouragement. Be careful, though, that an online forum isn't the only place where you express your feelings. Online communities and social media can become an echo chamber where we only surround ourselves with voices that sound similar to ours. We can begin to look for validation there that falls flat when we don't get the likes or attention we crave. Each of us needs real-life relationships where we can be heard, seen, and known. Even at their best, online connections can't offer us that.

You'll also want to be careful about when and what you share. Just as your grief deserves a trusted audience, grief isn't an experience that needs to be broadly public. Even if your ugly cries are private, they're still known by God. Even if your angry vents take place offline, they're still heard by the One who can actually do something about your problems. Hopefully you're already using discernment when it comes to what you post online. Use extra sensitivity when it comes to your grief. You can treat grief like the precious, delicate experience it is.

I'm afraid I'll forget my person. What should I do?

Rest assured—you will not forget your person! There might be memories of them that fade with time, but you will not forget entirely. Your brain is like a filing cabinet with endless drawers. Every single memory is stashed safely there, even the ones you won't be able to easily access.

However, leaving all the remembering up to your mind isn't a good idea. We have agenda books to remember our homework assignments, we have yearbooks to remember the school year, and we take pictures to remember fun moments. There are so many ways to record things we want to remember, and active remembering is a great way to grieve healthily and secure those memories for future comfort.

After our family's loss, we made photo albums, T-shirt quilts, and even pillowcases and T-shirts with our dad's picture on them. We still make desserts he loved and hang up pictures of us together around the house. Most of all, we tell stories about him—funny moments that we had with him and weird or quirky habits he had. We sit around and remember him together, and one person's memory jogs another person's. The task of carrying the memories is made lighter because we do it together.

Whether you enlist friends or family to help you remember or you capture your own memories, we encourage you to actively collect as many as you can. Here's a list of some things you could do to help remember your person:

- Use a piece of your loved one's clothing to make a pillowcase, wrap a book, or wear.
- Print out photos of you together and design a scrapbook or photo album.
- Make a playlist of their favorite songs or songs that remind you of them.
- Choose a picture of you together for your phone's wallpaper.
- Seek out activities that you enjoyed together.
- Get friends together specifically to share memories. Have someone record them.

- Cook their favorite food or visit a restaurant you enjoyed together.
- If your loved one died of an illness, run a 5K or sponsor a participant in an event that raises money for that health condition.
- Donate your time or money to a cause that was special for your person.
- Volunteer at an organization that supports families who grieve like yours.

While there are things that you might forget about the person you've lost, there are countless more ways to remember them. As you remember them in these tangible ways, use the experience to actively cement those memories into your mind. You won't remember everything, and that will always hurt. However, the memories that do stay will anchor you to your person and to their love for the rest of your life.

I want to feel happy again. How do I get there?

That's a great question! Not only do we hear that you want to get back to feeling joyful about life, but it's clear that you're willing to put in the work to get there. Therein is the secret: true contentment requires work.

While happiness flits around like a bumblebee, contentment has staying power. It brings satisfaction that actually sticks. As we work toward contentment, we discover there is something even deeper than happiness, which depends on our circumstances. Through God, joy is available to us after loss.

The apostle Paul tells the church in Philippi that the secret to his contentment is Christ. He says, "I have learned the secret of being content in any and every situation, whether well fed or hungry, whether living in plenty or in want. I can do all this through him who gives me strength."[21]

IN THEIR OWN WORDS: EMERSON'S STORY

I think the first time I experienced grief was when I was eight years old. My biological father moved out, and my parents got a divorce. When I was about thirteen, my mom brought a new man into our lives. His name was Stephen. When I first met Stephen, I wanted nothing to do with him. The thought of trusting another father was terrifying. Eventually, I let him in and my mom and Stephen got married. I realized that Stephen was not the same as my biological father; Stephen was kind, loving, funny, and he wanted to be a part of my life.

Less than a year after they got married, Stephen was diagnosed with cancer. It was the worst news ever: Stephen was the dad who chose to be in my life, and now I might lose him too. Stephen fought hard, but the cancer won. I had asked Stephen to adopt me a few months before, and although that was never completed, I view Stephen as my dad.

I have experienced lots of forms of grief, and it has taken a terrible toll on me. I miss my dad every day, but the grief has come in waves. Over time, I have gone through monumental moments without him here. I graduated from high school shortly after he passed, I went off to college, and I did it all without him standing with me. That was hard, scary, and totally unfair. I know that I will have a million more life events without him, and that stinks. I know I have more grief to process, and that stinks just as much. I am in college now, and some days I still don't have the courage to do much. Some days I just cry over how unfair it is that he isn't here.

—Emerson, age 18, reflecting on his dad's death a year and a half prior

For you, this strengthening may look like the power to get up in the morning and shower before school. It may sound like reaching out to a friend for encouragement on a hard day. Jesus' strengthening may look like a growing sense of joy when all you'd seen before were dark clouds of sorrow. Reach out to him, and in your weakness, he will display his resurrection power. This power can birth courage, hope, and peace—all of which can bring happiness to your life again.

After losing a loved one, most of us have to reorient how we think about happiness. We must look honestly at our lives and recognize that happiness is something we chase but contentment is something we cultivate. As we work to rebuild a life we love, we can trust that Jesus will give us strength to conquer every battle. We can rejoice in his power and love for us. It might take a while to be able to enjoy yourself again, but even in the mourning that you are experiencing, you can work toward lasting happiness in the joy and contentment that Jesus promises to give.

I actually feel fine. Is that okay?

Yes. Grief is different for everyone, and your journey through it is unique to you. If you're honest about your emotions and not attempting to run away from them, you can trust that feeling fine is, well, just fine! Let's consider some scenarios where "feeling fine" might be a very normal response to loss.

> If you had a complicated or hurtful relationship with the person who died, you might feel relieved that they are gone. For you, "fine" means a rest that wasn't there when the person was alive.
>
> If you had a distant relationship with the person who died, you might feel minimally sad that they're no longer around. Maybe they lived far away or you didn't know them very well. For you, "fine" means that you had a limited emotional connection to the person.
>
> If you watched your person die of a terminal illness, you might feel at peace knowing they are no longer in pain. For you, "fine" means that you understand this reality, and your process of letting go includes that understanding at the forefront.

"Fine" doesn't necessarily mean that you have zero emotions or that you're blocking out hard feelings, but we'll be honest—it's not an awesomely descriptive word either. As folks ask you how you're doing, consider using a word other than "fine" to help them understand what's going on inside of you. "I'm relieved." "I'm getting by." "I'm feeling at peace." They'll think you're super articulate, and you'll keep them from circling around and asking again!

4
THE BIG MAN
UPSTAIRS

In the center of a small New England town stands an old white general store locally known as Wayne's. The actual Wayne is long gone, but his memory and his love for good food live on in the little restaurant area on the sunny south end of the store. Next to a small counter with stools for diners, a bakery case glows, delicious homemade treats illuminated by the neon lights inside the cooler. Chocolate chip cookies bigger than two fists put together. Slices of blueberry pie. And our family's personal favorite: freshly made whoopie pies.

For the first year after our loss, I (Clarissa) took my kids to Wayne's every single Thursday after picking them up from school. I'd swing our old SUV through the school pickup line and then slip around the corner to park out front at Wayne's. We'd almost made it another week with grief, and it was time to celebrate that we were still surviving. I called those days "Whoopie Pie Thursdays." Sometimes we'd smile and enjoy the chocolate and icing-filled goodness, jabbering over the day's goings-on. Other times, after a particularly rough week, we'd eat mostly in silence. Through it all, Whoopie Pie Thursdays kept us hanging on.

Many people I talk to tell me they can't imagine how folks get through the pain of grief without God. They say, "I don't know how anybody can do this without Jesus." And while I agree with them that faith in Christ offers a light and hope that outshines every human encouragement, I want to be honest with you—walking with grief and God isn't always easy. God isn't a whoopie pie that fills your belly with happy feelings and gives you a sugar high. If you've been a Christian for any length of time, you know that living in relationship with God is far more complex than that. There are highs and lows, times of intimacy and moments where God feels far away. Faith isn't a sugar rush or endorphin hit to help you shoulder through hard seasons. On the contrary, it often shows up in ways you never expected once you experience a loss.

As Christians, we believe that your faith is an important part of your survival and flourishing after the death of a loved one. The truths of God's Word can give you comfort, encouragement, direction, and hope. But let's be very clear: faith's power after loss isn't about you holding on to God, clinging for dear life, battling for your belief in him. Instead, faith's power after loss is about God holding on to you. As you wrestle with big spiritual questions or as you experience apathy and doubt, God is holding on to you. As you rest in his love, this peace isn't something you create yourself. God is holding on to you. The late pastor and author Tim Keller put it this way: "It is not the strength of your faith but the object of your faith that actually saves you."[1]

We know that some days feel really good and others seem like you're barely hanging on. We understand that you need to choose your own Whoopie Pie Thursdays, little milestones and celebrations to mark that you're going to make it. We also know that, despite all of your good work engaging with your grief honestly, you can't get through it on your own. Your own strength isn't strong enough. But God's is. That's what this section is all about. We want you to know that your questions aren't too big for God. In fact, they're welcomed by him. Even the ones you aren't sure you could ever ask out loud.

LEARNING THE LANGUAGE OF FAITH IN GRIEF

Whether or not you're a Christian (or your loved one was), faith shows up at funerals. The finality of death makes us long for something transcendent. We realize we control far less than we thought, and we wonder who might have a hand on the steering wheel if we don't. The death of a loved one can prompt conversations, sometimes for the first time, about faith, spirituality, and God.

There's only one problem: most of us are not great at having these conversations. In our everyday lives, we're used to soliciting advice from YouTube tutorials or friends, not from the Bible. We're accustomed to "finding our own truth" rather than leaning into God's. This means that a lot of spiritual conversations, advice, and consolation after loss sound more like Hallmark cards than Bible verses. Even when Bible verses are used, they're distributed like fortune cookies or horoscope predictions. None of this offers much comfort. Most of it only provokes more questions.

We're convinced that it's super important to talk about God and faith after loss. We believe it's important to ask questions—honest ones, hard ones, and painful ones. We also know we don't have all the answers, and we encourage you to beware of anyone who does claim to have them.

For too long, Christians have worried that asking questions of our faith means we don't trust God or that our faith is weak. On the contrary, we're convinced that deeply faithful Christians ask a lot of questions. From time to time, they may doubt God's promises.

When life looks very dark, they may even wonder where God is. The key to faithful love for God isn't hush-hushing our biggest concerns and following blindly. Instead, when we bring our questions into his presence, God gives us exactly what we need every time. Not answers, necessarily, but something even better. He gives us his presence.

We're glad if you have questions about God and how to spiritually make sense of your loss. In this chapter, we've tried to address the questions teens ask most, including some that might sound a little heretical to you! If you're struggling with your faith, we're here to affirm and encourage you, not convince you. Wrestling with belief is normal after loss.

On the flip side, if you're finding great comfort in your faith, we're here to cheer you on, not to make you start to question the ground under your feet. Finally, if you're not sure that God even exists, we're especially glad you're reading this book. The death of a loved one can offer an important opportunity to think critically about your life—what matters, where you're going, and who you want to walk with you. We're convinced that these are spiritual questions too, and that they deserve your attention.

YOUR QUESTIONS ANSWERED

Is God mad at me? Is this my fault? Did this happen because I sinned?

We live in a world of cause and effect. We're fascinated by it, actually. As little kids, we line up dominoes in a row just to knock them down and watch them cascade across the floor. As teenagers, we shake up cans of soda and then hand them to a friend just to see what will happen when they open them! It makes sense, then, that when it comes to loss, we look for a cause that led to the effect of death.

GOD GRIEVES TOO[2]

OLD TESTAMENT

Before sending the Flood, God grieves that people have rejected him (see Genesis 6:6).

God grieves that Israel disobeys him during their forty years of wilderness wandering (see Psalm 78:40).

God grieves when he sees Israel bear the consequences of its disobedience (see Judges 10:16).

Isaiah prophesies that the Messiah will experience grief and pain (see Isaiah 53:3).

NEW TESTAMENT

Jesus weeps at Lazarus's tomb (see John 11:33-35).

Jesus grieves for Jerusalem as he approaches the city on a donkey (see Luke 19:41).

Jesus is overwhelmed with sorrow in the garden of Gethsemane before his death (see Matthew 26:38).

Unfortunately—and fortunately—it's not that simple. While many causes and effects make sense in this world, others defy our understanding. We know that cancer kills a body by replicating unhealthy cells throughout it, but well-trained scientists in labs can't tell you precisely why some people get sick and others don't. We can figure out many cause-effect relationships in the physical world, but when it comes to God, we're mostly left with mystery.

In ancient cultures, disabilities and illnesses were seen as the punishment of the gods, and many Jews in Jesus' day believed that Yahweh, the God of Israel, acted in similar ways. If God was happy with them, they enjoyed physical health. If God was displeased with them, they believed he would bring down judgment in crippling ways.

The Gospel of John tells the story of Jesus' disciples wrestling with these ancient beliefs and the presence of God in brokenness. They met a man who had been born blind, and the disciples were convinced that God was mad at this man or his family. Someone had done something wrong to make this bad thing happen.

Jesus explained it differently. He said, "You're asking the wrong question. You're looking for someone to blame. There is no such cause-effect here."[3]

We'll be honest: sometimes our loved ones' poor choices lead to their deaths. Sometimes sin seems easily identifiable. For example, if your loved one died because of substance abuse or participated in criminal activity that led to death, sin may be a deeply sad part of their ending. However, even here, Jesus' conversation with his disciples warns us against quickly judging the situation. We see only from our human perspective; God sees so much more.

As we look at the character of God—almighty, just, holy, loving, merciful, wise, and good—we're convinced that your person's death is not a result of God's anger or punishment in your life but of the brokenness of this world. Your person's death isn't your fault. Your sin did not make them die. Instead, Romans 5:12 tells us that, through one person's sin, death entered the world. Your person died because this world has been falling apart since the fatal bite of fruit in the Garden of Eden. Death falls like rain on the just and the unjust, a terrible thing that happens both to those who love God and to those who give him no attention.[4]

This, of course, raises the question, *If it's not my fault, why did this happen?* Here we must become content with mystery. Jesus told his disciples that the man's blindness offered an opportunity for him to seek God. "Look . . . for what God can do," Jesus said.[5] We can generally accept that we and our loved ones die because of sin's pervasiveness in the world, but we still long to understand the specifics. Why did *my* person die? This we must leave to mystery.

Scripture tells us that God knows the number of our days (see Psalm 139:16). He writes the story of our lives before we've put a single word on the page. In God's economy, there is no one who dies "too soon" because he knows the length of each life and has ordained its goodness. God stands beyond time and sees the whole movie of our lives, while we only see a freeze-frame. This, perhaps, is the hardest part of reckoning with death. When it comes to our loss, there are some things that (in this life) we will just never know. They are beyond our understanding.

When we're faced with *why* questions, it helps to do just what Jesus told his disciples to do: look to God. When we are puzzled, we can trust his character—his wisdom, justice, and mercy. When we are frustrated, we can lean into his comfort, his strength, and his peace. The Bible tells us that God works all things together for good.[6] But it never tells us we'll understand this working in our lifetimes. Until we're face-to-face with Jesus and can get our questions answered, God asks us to look at him and know that, in all things, his heart is for us.

Is God actually good and loving?

Throughout the Bible, we can find many examples of God's unending faithfulness and love to his people. He rescued them from their enemies countless times, led them through the desert to their own land even when they complained about it, and sent his Son to die for the world. But even with this great track record, it's easy to look at your own life and wonder if God is still working for *your* good.

The death of a loved one breaks the illusion that if you live a good life and try to do what's right, you'll always experience blessing, peace, and happiness. It brings you face-to-face with your powerlessness. This lack of control can make you question who is actually calling the shots in this world. You might reason that a good God wouldn't allow bad things to happen to basically good people.

Loss exposes this kind of transactional thinking that even people who love Jesus are prone to believe. We know that good deeds don't secure our salvation, but we might secretly believe that they're certainly helpful. We read in the Bible that God blesses those who are faithful to him, but we fail to realize that the blessings God offers often look different than the deliveries of happiness we'd like to receive.

We want you to know that it's okay to question God's love and goodness. Your doubts right now aren't a sign of weak faith. Instead, we see them as testing the ropes. Here's what we mean.

We live less than ten miles from the Atlantic Ocean, so we see a lot of boaters around us. Folks rent space at wharves and marinas along the rivers that run to the ocean, and all summer long the waterways buzz with activity.

If you head down to the marina on a Saturday late afternoon, you'll see boaters returning from their days on the water. They navigate their crafts into their rented spaces, and a passenger hops out onto the dock and grabs the rope they're thrown from the boat. Wrapping it once, twice, three times in a figure-eight pattern around the dock cleat, the person moors the boat securely to the dock. And then, before everyone disembarks and heads home, he does one last important thing: he tugs the rope tied at the cleat, testing it for its strength.

Your questions about God's goodness and love test the ropes of your faith. You may have already moored yourself to Jesus through faith in his death for you, but the storms of life have made you wonder if you're still secure. If you're just starting to investigate the claims of Jesus, this might be your first encounter with the idea of a loving God. Either way, loss has caused you to question whether the truths that held you before can still be trusted. Your questions tug at those ropes that connect you and God. No matter how hard you pull, you'll find God's character unchanged and totally secure every time.

As you test the ropes of God's goodness and love, we encourage you to keep your eyes on Jesus. As the image of the invisible God, Jesus shows us exactly what God is like.[7] Not sure if God is still good and loving? Just look at Jesus. John 15:13 says, "Greater love has no one than this: to lay down one's life for one's friends." Jesus did exactly that! Death didn't stop him from loving. In fact, he faced it head-on so that he could call us friends. We were left with no way to earn the status "child of God" because of our sin, so Jesus chose us in love. He was willing to face death in all its pain and horror specifically because he loved you.

Is this all the answer you need? It may or may not be. Just because we know something to be true doesn't mean we feel it. Here's where our boat analogy is helpful again. If you've tied your ropes to the cleats carefully, if you've checked to make sure they're tight, it may simply be time to walk down that dock and trust that your boat won't float away. In the same way, if you've tugged at the ropes of God's goodness and love, if you've gone to Scripture for reassurance of his character, it may simply be time to trust and step forward into your life with Jesus by your side. Whether you've loved God for years or spiritual things are all new to you, we're convinced that in time you'll find Jesus to be more beautiful and loving than you ever imagined.

VERSES TO REMEMBER

It's easy to feel like there's nobody who gets how hard life with grief really is. Thankfully, our all-knowing, all-wise, all-loving God does! Tuck these verses away in your heart. Write them in your day planner or take a picture of this page so that you'll have these words from God to you. We all need reminders of his love, his power, and his presence.

When you feel like nobody understands...

> He was despised and rejected—a man of sorrows, acquainted with deepest grief.... It was our weaknesses he carried; it was our sorrows that weighed him down.
> ISAIAH 53:3-4, NLT

> You keep track of all my sorrows. You have collected all my tears in your bottle. You have recorded each one in your book.
> PSALM 56:8, NLT

When you feel like nobody cares...

> Give all your worries and cares to God, for he cares about you.
> 1 PETER 5:7, NLT

> He heals the brokenhearted and binds up their wounds. He determines the number of the stars and calls them each by name.
> PSALM 147:3-4

When you feel like nobody can help...

> If your heart is broken, you'll find GOD right there; if you're kicked in the gut, he'll help you catch your breath.
> PSALM 34:18, MSG

> Jesus said, "Come to me, all of you who are weary and carry heavy burdens, and I will give you rest. Take my yoke upon you. Let me teach you, because I am humble and gentle at heart, and you will find rest for your souls. For my yoke is easy to bear, and the burden I give you is light."
> MATTHEW 11:28-30, NLT

When you feel like you're all alone...

When you go through deep waters, I will be with you. When you go through rivers of difficulty, you will not drown. When you walk through the fire of oppression, you will not be burned up; the flames will not consume you.
ISAIAH 43:2, NLT

God goes with you; he will never leave you nor forsake you.
DEUTERONOMY 31:6

When you're not sure what the future holds...

I know what I'm doing. I have it all planned out—plans to take care of you, not abandon you, plans to give you the future you hope for.
JEREMIAH 29:11, MSG

You, LORD, are all I have, and you give me all I need; my future is in your hands.
PSALM 16:5, GNT

What should I think about the afterlife?

Since ancient times, people have believed in a life after death. (It's actually sort of a modern invention to believe that nothing exists after we die.) God placed within us a longing for eternal communion with him, and every religion in one way or another has tried to create an image of what life after death might look like.[8]

When it comes to thinking about heaven and the afterlife, we need to be careful to separate what the Bible tells us from what religious folklore says. Contrary to cartoons, movies, and memes, there is no indication that after we die we sit on clouds, play harps, and engage in practical jokes on those who "live below" on earth. The Bible is also pretty clear that our deceased loved ones don't send us messages from the afterlife.[9]

While the Bible doesn't give us a photographic image of what life after death is like, we do know these things about where believers go after death and what they do:

- For those who trust in Jesus, to be absent from our bodies is to be present with God (see 2 Corinthians 5:8).
- Jesus has prepared a place for us to enjoy his presence forever (see John 14:2 and 2 Corinthians 5:1).
- The presence of Jesus is paradise for us (see Luke 23:43).
- Those who have died in faith are cheering us on in a "great cloud of witnesses" as we live for Jesus (see Hebrews 12:1).

But it doesn't end there. Yes, our loved ones will die; and yes, we will also die. But Jesus is alive! His resurrected body is the preview of our resurrection! Will you one day see your loved one again? Yes, through faith in God's redemptive goodness, you will. However, it gets even better than that. One day, when Jesus comes again, he will make everything new—you, me, our loved ones, the mountains and animals, the trees and oceans. All creation will one day marvel at this transformation. Heaven isn't the finish line for Christians, then. We await a greater hope. For those who love God, there is, as author N. T. Wright puts it, "life *after* 'life after death.'"[10]

While, again, the Bible doesn't give us a photographic image of what this new creation will be like, we do know these things for sure:

- When Jesus comes again, he will transform our broken bodies into gloriously new ones (see Philippians 3:20-21).
- Grief, pain, and crying will be nonexistent (see Revelation 21:4).
- The beauty and perfection of the new creation will boggle our minds (see 1 Corinthians 2:9).
- Peace will replace conflict, and abundance will replace scarcity (see Revelation 22:1-3).

- Every wrong will be righted by God, who rules justly (see 2 Peter 3:13).
- We will know God fully, face-to-face (see Revelation 22:4).
- Joyful praise will always be on our lips as we enjoy fellowship with each other (see Revelation 7:9-12).

C. S. Lewis wrote to his dying friend Mary, "There are better things ahead than any we leave behind."[11] According to Scripture, these are the joys that await those who die in faith, trusting Jesus. If your loved one was a Christian, you can trust with confidence that God will fulfill all of his promises—that your person is safe in Jesus' care now and that one day you'll enjoy eternity together, praising God in the renewed, restored creation that he loved into existence.

What if I don't know what my person thought about God?

The Bible tells us that those who choose not to trust in Jesus eventually receive the life they have always desired—one apart from God. This is a hard reality and should spur us on to share the good news of God's love with everyone we meet. However, we need not take this truth as an opportunity for discouragement layered onto our grief. Here's why.

As Jesus hung on the cross, a man hanging beside him called out for grace.[12] Side by side on their crosses, only hours from their own deaths, that short conversation changed the man's eternal destiny. Did the man's loved ones know about it? We're not told. What we do know is that Jesus' grace covered this man's sin and redeemed his heart even at that late hour of his life.

As we commit our loved ones to God's care, we can hold on to the truth that God desires each person to come to know him and that he seeks them out, even as they are dying.[13] It can be really hard to leave our loved ones' eternal destinies to God. Nonetheless, we can entrust even this to him, knowing that he is wise, just, and merciful.

What should I pray? I don't feel like I have words to say what I feel.

Sometimes prayer is hard. We don't know what to say or don't want to say anything at all. That's okay. God wants to hear from you no matter what.

The book of Psalms is a collection of prayers that can help us when we want to talk to God. We often think we have to be thankful or happy when we pray, but the Bible offers a very different approach. In addition to praising God, the psalms include complaints, groans, and shouts at God. Some psalms are long, angry venting to God.

The psalms show us that true faith brings every part of our lives to God; we don't have to only present our good side. Instead of ignoring God or taking our troubles elsewhere, we can turn to him. Your prayers don't have to have a particular format. You don't even need to say amen. You can sit in silence and bring your feelings to God. The great mystic theologian and monk Thomas Merton once said, "My God, I pray better to You by breathing. I pray better to You by walking than by talking."[14] Maybe you feel the same right now. Even when you have no words, God understands everything you're thinking and feeling.

We have included many prayers in this book to help you talk to God about how you're feeling. You can also ask a friend to pray for you if you can't do it yourself. You can pray out loud, in your head, in a journal, or with someone else. It doesn't matter how you do it! You can use already-written prayers, worship music, art, dance, or music to express yourself to God. The important thing is to keep the lines of communication open. God stands ready to listen and love you, even when the words don't seem to come.

I don't want to go to church anymore. Do I have to keep going?

After my dad died, my family didn't go to church consistently for a long time. On some Sundays, a few of us would want to go but others

PRAYER

God, sometimes, I confess, it's hard to believe you're still here. If I had the choice, I would have left long ago. Thank you for sticking by me, for promising never to leave me, especially when life's road gets hard. Jesus, remind me that you understand my sadness. Holy Spirit, give me your comfort. Heavenly Father, when I start to feel like you've abandoned me, draw me close and assure me of your never-ending love. Amen.

wouldn't. Sometimes we were just too tired from trying to make it through the week with grief. Other times, grief felt like an awkward visitor that we didn't really want to bring along with us. My mom cried *a lot* whenever we went to church, and that was awkward too. It would have been easy to give up going altogether.

After your person dies, church might feel like a hard place to go back to. We are used to vulnerability at church through worship and prayer. Bringing our new raw vulnerabilities into a congregation can feel risky, especially if your church is the kind that mostly focuses on upbeat worship and loud praise. Seeing other people praising when you're hurting can really pinch.

Just like all the other ways you're learning to navigate life with grief, you need to learn when to lean in and when to let go. You may need to start with only Sunday school or youth group before attending a large Sunday morning service, just to get comfortable again in the space and around those people. If your loss is shared by your church community, you may find comfort from meeting outside of Sunday church time to start. As with all reentries after loss, we encourage you to go slowly. Some Sundays, you may need to stay home and take a break. Jesus understands that this is hard.

As you lean in, you'll find that church sometimes feels very uncomfortable. Praise falls painfully on your ears when you only want to lament, and Bible verses may bring tears as you remember your person. You may struggle to believe Scripture's truths that once were easy to accept.

But church is exactly the place to bring all these mixed emotions. We can bring our whole selves to God, so all of our brokenness, questions, and feelings are welcome in worship. Don't look around and assume everybody else has it all together. Instead, as you participate at church, begin to look at the people in your congregation as fellow grievers. Everybody is bringing something hard to church—a divorce, a broken friendship, a health problem. We're all coming to be seen and heard and healed by the Great Physician, who promises us peace for our hurting souls, forgiveness for our sins, and abundant life to give us joy.

The writer of Hebrews encouraged the church not to give up meeting together.[15] Each of us needs encouragement and support for our life's journey, and you will find that when you gather as part of the church. Even if it takes a long time or comes in fits and starts, don't give up on church. It's the community Jesus loved and lived and died for, and your presence in it is indispensable.

Why isn't my church helping?

We're so sorry that your church community hasn't stepped forward to care for you since your person died. (We're going to assume that they know. If they don't, be sure to tell them! They can't help what they don't know about.) While the church is the special gathering of those who love Jesus, we are an imperfect bunch. Too often, the church doesn't live or look the way it's supposed to.

While we don't know the specific reasons your church hasn't proactively offered the support you need, we're convinced that it could. You could actually be the perfect guide. Here's what we recommend. First, set up a time to talk with a person on your church's staff, like a youth group leader or pastor. Instead of complaining, arrive ready to talk about what you—and other grieving people in your community—need. Could you use help with meals at your house? Does the lawn really need mowing, or do you need rides so you can get to school events? Share what practical needs you have and ask for help. You're not the first person who has needed care after a loss, and your pastoral staff is well trained to coordinate that kind of support.

Second, talk to your pastor or youth leader about what your heart needs as you grieve and return to church. Do you need extra space in the church service for silence? Could the pastor include a prayer of lament to give words to your—and others'—pain? Would you appreciate healing prayer, a small group for students going through loss, or a mentor or prayer partner?

No, many churches don't do a great job of caring for grieving people, but we're convinced that, with a little help, they can get better at it. Perhaps God can use your pain to open up doors of comforting care for you and many others who participate in your congregation. You might be surprised to see that improvements begin when you ask for what you need.

I don't really care about God anymore. Does that matter?

It's normal to have ambivalent feelings about God after your loved one dies. While some people find their faith strengthened after a loss, others feel like everything begins to wobble. You might even feel like death has made you question everything, to the point of walking away from God entirely.

Jesus' disciple John wrote to the church, "We love because he first loved us."[16] Did you catch the order there? God went first. Even when your questions loom largest, God has gone first. He has loved you since before time began, and his love won't stop even if you feel like yours has run out.

Does it matter, then, if you don't care about God anymore? Yes, it does. God longs for you with a mother's love.[17] He's written your name on the palms of his hands.[18] God waits for you like the father waits for his prodigal son to return.[19] He's got a banquet ready for you on your arrival. Jesus stands knocking at the door, persistently pursuing a loving relationship with you.[20] He wants to enjoy your presence. As you wrestle with thoughts and feelings about God, we encourage you to keep talking to him—even if it's an "I don't care about you anymore." Because he loved you first, God's not going to give up on you.

I prayed for my person to be healed, but he still died. Did God answer "no"?

A lot of Christians will tell you that God answered "yes" to your prayer by providing ultimate healing, alleviating your person's pain and sickness by taking your loved one to heaven. It might surprise you, but I (Clarissa) am not going to tell you this. In fact, I believe that's a really dangerous answer to an awfully complicated question. That kind of reasoning—that God takes our prayers and reinterprets the words into what he wants instead—makes prayer an untrustworthy business. How can I know what words to pray if I'm not sure God will choose to hear them the way I intend them?

God is at his essence a communicator, and he understands the plain meaning of our words when we speak to him. He understood that you were praying for *physical* healing for your loved one. You wanted your person's cancer to disappear. You wanted his frailty and sickness to be replaced with a life renewed in vigor and health. You weren't praying, "God, please take my person home to be with you and heal him in that way." God knows this, and I do too.

To your question, then, it would seem the answer is painfully clear—God answered "no." Here is where "spiritual" answers like the ones you often hear fall flat. Because a "no" from God is hard to receive. It's shrouded in mystery. A "no" comes along with a million *why* questions that won't be answered in this life. You can try to reason yourself out of disappointment when it comes to other "no"

IN THEIR OWN WORDS: RACHEL'S STORY

I lost both my grandparents on my dad's side three weeks apart from each other from COVID-19. I questioned, and still do, why they were taken from me so soon and during the holidays. No holiday has ever been the same. I have moments that I forget they are gone and think, *I should call Mawmaw,* and then remember that I can't. Every day when I wake up, there is always a split second where I don't remember they are gone, and then that second is over and I'm sad again.

I constantly try to bargain with God to get them back. *If I just had them for a minute. If I could get a hug. If she could tell me it would be okay.* I have many regrets that are heavy weights on my heart since they passed. And truly, I think it's even harder because they died when COVID-19 was rampant. There was no saying "Goodbye" or "I love you" one last time. They were just gone. I have cried so much, I can't cry anymore. I'm just numb.

—Rachel, age 20, whose grandfather and grandmother died three years prior

answers. For example, God must have a better college in store for me; that's why he didn't answer my prayer after I submitted my application hoping for acceptance. But you can't do that with loss. It makes no sense to say, "God must have a better dad in store for me; that's why he didn't heal my dad when I prayed."

First, I want you to know that Jesus understands what it means to receive a "no." In the garden of Gethsemane, he asked God to change his coming suffering, to call the whole dying on the cross thing off. But God said no. God had plans to work all things for our good, and for Jesus, that meant accepting a path through suffering. Later, on the cross, Jesus would know the silence of God in a way we will never experience. Jesus gets how hard it is to walk by faith when we can't see what God is doing.

In moments like these and in the face of questions like these, we are left to grieve the giant gap between our wisdom and God's and to throw ourselves fully onto his amazing character. Though we don't understand God's ways, we can know his heart—his goodness, faithfulness, and lovingkindness. We can trust that his wisdom is higher and better than our own. We can choose to believe that he is always for us, even when the answer is "no." Part of walking with grief is learning to hold two conflicting emotions in tension—joy and sorrow, despair and hope. Here, God asks us to do something similar, holding in tension our desires and his mysterious, sovereign plans.

What's the purpose in all of this?

You might feel like you are in exile right now. Taken from your normal life, you have been shoved into a world where sadness and grief seem to reign over you. It is hard to see the bigger picture when death has messed up everything. We get it. Sometimes a greater purpose is incredibly hard to find.

We may never know God's purposes for our particular sufferings in this life. Job didn't receive clarity about his trials; neither did the apostle Paul. Hannah never learned why it took so long for her desperate prayers for a baby to be answered. Mary and Martha didn't get a straight answer on why their brother Lazarus died. Nevertheless, God assures us that our "problems and trials . . . help us develop endurance. And endurance develops strength of character, and character strengthens our confident hope of salvation. And this hope will not lead to disappointment."[21]

God told the exiled nation of Israel, "For my thoughts are not your thoughts, neither are your ways my ways . . . As the heavens are higher than the earth, so are my ways higher than your ways and my thoughts than your thoughts."[22] Our heavenly Father asks us to trust that he can see things we can't and is using even our suffering to make us more like him. When we don't know what's going on, we can be confident that God does.

5

WHEN GRIEF IS OLD NEWS

We've all heard it said that fame lasts fifteen minutes. Lunch meat in your fridge lasts a little bit longer—three to five days.[1] Grief, on the other hand, can last a lot longer. The funny thing about grief, though, is that it doesn't easily fade like fame or grow extra stinky like leftover honey ham. As time passes, grief tends to linger quietly in the background, revealing itself in moments when you might not expect it.

Eventually grief becomes old news—for your friends, for your family, even for you. You want to think about other things and talk about other things, even though you still carry around this hole in your heart. This is a normal part of growing up with grief as a teenager. Lord willing, you have a lot of life left to live, and adolescence means you're thinking a lot about that life. God has built resilience into your body, mind, and heart; and as the days and months and years pass, you will learn to live with your grief.

Paul writes to the church in Rome that all of creation lives in this now-and-not-yet season. We're all groaning, he says, waiting for God to show up and fulfill his promises.[2] There's an aching that we've become accustomed to as we hold out hope. This is what life looks like when grief isn't new anymore: a mix of hope and sadness, looking forward and looking back, growth and grief with a whole lot of God's grace poured out over you.

Your love for your person didn't end when he or she died. Your grief won't end either. In one way or another, you will always miss your person, whether that's just occasional twinges when you remember him or her or an abiding longing that will only be eased when Jesus comes again. But that doesn't mean that your life can't be good and happy and fulfilling. On the contrary, when grief settles into your heart's home and unpacks its suitcases, you have a real opportunity to live authentically in this world, showing forth the goodness of God and trusting him for what you can't control.

CHANGE IS CAN BE GOOD

Change can be disconcerting, especially change we didn't ask for. You may find that as grief shape-shifts in your life, you feel disarmed by the changes. You kind of got used to being sad all the time, only to discover that you don't feel that way anymore. You don't think about your person very much, but special moments provoke those old emotions and make them feel fresh. Maybe the emotions you first associated with grief—anger, sadness, frustration—have melted into new, softer emotions such as peace, happiness, and hopeful anticipation. You think maybe you're done with grief altogether.

As you engage with your grief instead of running away from it, you'll find that these changes are healthy. You can welcome them. They are evidence that you're doing the hard work of facing your loss and learning to live again. Because we know that grief isn't just sadness, we can welcome these new feelings and the new experiences that come with them as part of grief too. Grief offers us wisdom on how to live better. It gives us renewed perspective and enthusiasm for what lies before us. Grief carries with it hidden gifts. Over time, the changes we experience manifest these gifts in our lives.

In this section, we want to help you begin to think about life when grief is no longer new. When the dust settles after the funeral and you've gone back to school. When you're "used to" (as "used to" as you'll ever get) not seeing your person every day. There will come a time when grief's sharp pains shift into a duller ache, and this shift will bring all kinds of new questions. We hope to address them here.

Each person's journey with grief will look unique. You may find that grief starts to feel familiar a few months after your loss, while for someone else it may take years for grief to feel like old news. Both are valid responses to loss. Regardless of how long it takes for your life to open up again, we want you to know this: you're going to make it. Grief won't always be *the* thing that defines your life. Someday, you'll find that grief is only a part of who you are. God will bring you through your valley of the shadow to rest by quiet waters and to feast again at his table of goodness.

YOUR QUESTIONS ANSWERED

Is the first year the hardest? Will it get better with time?

Many times, people say the first year is the hardest because you have to adjust to the reality of living without your person. You're fumbling around, bumping into big emotions because you've never experienced them before. However, grief is not linear! There is no way to predict how you will feel or when the sadness will ease up. Some days the distance that time creates is a comfort, and others it seems like a barrier you are always trying to climb over. When you reach the one-year anniversary of your person's death, you may experience a

SELF-CHECK: PAST, PRESENT, OR FUTURE

Each day is different when you're grieving. And as crazy as it might sound, sometimes each day *also* feels the same, like you're living in a weird time warp. It can be hard to figure out where you are and where you're headed. Look below to see where you might be at today!

You might be feeling past-oriented today if . . .
- ☐ You're scrolling through old text threads.
- ☐ You set your phone wallpaper to a picture of you and your person.
- ☐ You wish you could stay in bed.
- ☐ You find your mind drifting to the way things used to be.
- ☐ Your bedroom looks the same as it did before your person died.

You might be feeling present-oriented today if . . .
- ☐ Off the top of your head, you can't remember how many days/ months it has been since your person died.
- ☐ You're really focused on getting ready for today's big test.
- ☐ You've got a long text thread going with friends about this weekend's plans.
- ☐ You can't go to sleep until you've read the next chapter in your book. It's *that* good!
- ☐ You wonder what's on the menu for dinner tonight.

sense of relief that you've made it this far or increased sorrow as you see time separate you further from your person.

Honestly, each year brings its own challenges. The first year, you adjust to reality. The second year, you adjust to the changes. The third year, you realize how much time is passing. Every year requires that you face your loss in new ways.

Fearing what year will be the hardest is a symptom of linear thinking, and we encourage you to regularly remind yourself of this. Instead, make a conscious choice to dedicate each month or year (however you're counting time) to God. We've learned that even though you can't count on feelings to be consistent, you can count on God. If you feel hopeless, God is there to give you hope and rest.

You might be feeling future-oriented today if . . .

- ☐ You're counting down the days till the next school break.
- ☐ You sometimes think about what you want to do after you graduate.
- ☐ It makes you sad to think of your person not being at your wedding.
- ☐ You get frustrated because you're not sure what the future holds.
- ☐ You are thinking of rearranging the furniture in your room.
- ☐ You google to see when the next Taylor Swift album is coming out.

Count up your check marks. Do you notice that you've got more in one category than another? Are your thoughts and feelings evenly distributed across past, present, and future? What could you add to the category where you have the most checked boxes? How does it make you feel to categorize your thoughts and feelings in this way?

Remember that your life with grief will shift from day to day and season to season. The way you feel today may not be the way you feel in two weeks. After a hard day at school, your outlook might change. After a good talk with a friend, it might change again. In the end, learning to live with grief isn't about moving along a timeline to get over your feelings. Instead, we grow with grief as we take notice of our emotions, treat them gently and kindly, and offer ourselves the care and encouragement we need to take our next steps in hope.

If you feel joyful, he is right alongside you. No matter your circumstance, God will meet you and fulfill everything that concerns you. You can trust that he will stay faithful for all the years to come.

My person won't be there at my graduation. How do I handle that?

Milestones often make grief feel bigger. You are wise to anticipate that you might encounter some big emotions the day you graduate from high school. Big emotions may also show up before or after your birthday, your high school prom, or family gatherings. How do you handle it when your person won't be there to help you get ready, psych you up before the big test, or cheer you on from the bleachers?

Grief researchers have proposed a theory called "continuing bonds" that might be helpful to you in these moments.[3] Instead of death severing the relationship we have with our person, these researchers observed that relationships of love still continue after loss. They just take different forms. For example, you might have enjoyed listening to your grandpa's funny stories when he was alive. Now you retell them to your friends as a way of connecting with his memory and loving him in his absence. You're continuing and even enhancing the relational bond you had with your grandpa as you invite his life into your life.

How will you do this at graduation? Maybe you'll choose to wear your uncle's tie underneath your graduation gown, a tangible reminder on your body that his love travels with you wherever you go. Maybe you'll have a good cry the night before prom to release those emotions and let your body acknowledge the pain of your person's absence. Maybe you'll simply smile knowingly as you open your birthday gifts, imagining your person's pleasure. You may do these things in the weeks prior, on the day of, or even after the festivities are over. Attentiveness like this anchors you in who you are and the love that has brought you to this moment.

Milestones aren't easy to face without the people we love, but even your courage to face these events is a testimony to your love for your person. You love them so much that you're committed to creatively bringing them into the life you lead without them—even if you do it with tears in your eyes or a lump in your throat.

What do I do if my parent wants to remarry?

You probably feel like your life is fine the way it is or that it's screwed up enough without your mom or dad getting remarried. Maybe you feel a mixture of both. As someone whose mom has gotten remarried, I (Fiona) am here to tell you that all those feelings are okay. You can be mad, scared, happy, and anything in between. The death of a parent affects our feelings about the future in general, and it brings specific concerns about what that future could look like.

When my mom told my siblings and me that she was getting married, I had a lot of mixed feelings. I was excited for my mom because she was really happy. Now she wouldn't be alone when the four of us kids went off to college. However, I also felt dread because I did not want our family to change again. More than a year later, I still sometimes have those feelings. But I can see the way that God is working even in a situation that I might not have thought I needed.

If and when your family goes through this change, there are two important things to remember: your stepdad or stepmom doesn't replace the parent you lost, and building relationships is important even when you don't want to.

First of all, if your parent remarries, their new spouse does not replace the parent you lost. Regardless of your parent's intention in marrying again, a new stepparent cannot fill the hole in your heart. My mom's husband is a wonderful person, but he doesn't have to be equal to who my dad was to me. It's not fair to him if I always measure him against my dad. Neither is it helpful for me to expect the same relationship. If your parent remarries, their new spouse may become a friend or great companion to you, or they might remain a polite acquaintance. However that relationship develops over time, don't ever feel like someone new must replace the parent you loved and lost.

Second, take active steps to build a relationship. Whether or not you like your stepparent, it is really hard to build a relationship after loss. All relationships take time and effort. If you're grieving, you may not want to invest in someone new. Even the attempt might bring mixed emotions as you wrestle with your feelings about the parent you've lost and the finality of their absence.

Because we know family changes literally take years to adjust into new normals, we encourage you to take a no-pressure approach. Try to connect with the new adult in your parent's life when you can. Don't push yourself to be extra engaging; simply work on being genuine. It's okay to check out sometimes, to need your space, to feel all the big emotions that come along with change. Alongside that extra gentleness with yourself, though, remember that if you want to have a good relationship with anyone, you have to be willing to cultivate it. You have to put in the work. If you don't have a good relationship with your parent, start there first. Connecting more deeply with your parent may help you to grow to accept this change and eventually embrace it.

Will I ever be able to drive by where the accident happened?

From the time you were a little kid, you've associated yourself with places. You memorized your street address. You learned to navigate your neighborhood on your bike. You may have moved and had to reestablish who you were in relation to your new location. When someone asks you, "Where are you from?" you're reminded that places matter.

Grief makes certain places harder to visit than others. You once may have had mostly happy memories related to places, but now you've got intensely painful ones too. If your loved one spent a lot of time in the hospital, doctor's offices and hospitals may prompt painful memories. You might even feel physically sick—nauseous or emotionally drained—when you think of these spots. If your person died in an accident, you may want to avoid ever going near the place where their death happened. To your confusion, you may also find that you feel strangely drawn to visit the place where your person's life ended, while at the same time feeling scared of it. All of these responses after loss are normal.

Because we draw so much identity from places, you are wise to think about your person's location of death as a part of your grieving.

5 WAYS . . .

TO HELP YOU MAKE PEACE WITH THE PAST, EMBRACE THE PRESENT, AND RELEASE THE FUTURE INTO GOD'S HANDS

1. WRITE A LETTER TO YOUR PERSON . . .

. . . about a past problem. Say what needs to be said. *"I love you. I'm sorry. I forgive you."*

. . . about your life today. What's going on with you? Catch them up.

. . . about your future. Have you given up dreaming? When will you miss your person? Tell them where you feel those holes in your life.

2. LISTEN TO A SONG THAT . . .

. . . describes how you felt right after your person died. How does the music take you back?

. . . describes how you feel today, at this moment. What emotions do you notice?

. . . reminds you of God's promises to you—for today and for your future. Where do you notice hope?

3. FIND A PICTURE OF YOURSELF . . .

. . . from when you were a little kid. Boy, have you grown! You're so different now.

. . . with your person. Retell your heart the story of the photo.

. . . where you're doing something goofy. Grief lives alongside laughter. Crack a smile just to remind your body that sorrow isn't the only thing that exists inside you.

4. VISIT A PLACE THAT . . .

. . . reminds you of your person. (This doesn't need to be a place you actually visited with them.)

. . . tells you something about your identity/who you are. Why did you choose this place?

. . . gives you peace. Take some deep cleansing breaths. God is here with you.

5. CONNECT WITH A PERSON WHO . . .

. . . you've known for a long time. Try to calculate together how long you've known each other. How long has it been in minutes, days, months, or years?

. . . has also been or is going through something hard. Let them know you care about them.

. . . reminds you that you're loved. This could be a friend, relative, teacher, coach, youth pastor, or therapist.

Must you go back to where your person died? Maybe not. Perhaps you can avoid it for the rest of your life. *Should* you go back to where your person died? It all depends. As you discern whether to return to the hospital or the site of the accident, consider putting into place these important supports:

First, make a plan. Do you need to drop by on the spur of the moment, or would it be easier to think about your visit in advance? Do you want to bring something to leave in memory of your person (a small rock, a flower, a note, etc.)?

Second, don't try this alone. You don't know how you'll respond in the moment, so take someone with you. Your support person can sit in the car, wait at the door, or walk with you—whatever you need at that moment. If you feel you need to go on your own, let a trusted adult know where you're headed and why. Check in afterward with them to debrief.

Finally, watch for the ordinary. Places possess power because of memory, but they're still just places. If you decide to visit your important location, pay attention to the ordinary life that continues in that spot. Watch the cars at the intersection that pass through unharmed. Take a deep breath and smell the fragrant shrubs that line the walkway into the doctor's office. Engage your thinking brain and count the windows on the hospital. When you do these things, you will slowly begin to release the painful power the location has over your heart.

Will it always be hard to visit the place where your person died? Maybe. You may only ever want to visit once. You may find it helpful simply to visit in your mind. Or you might find that as you visit over and over again, you discover a sense of closeness with your person in this spot that once brought only pain. Whatever you choose, know that there is no right and wrong here. All that matters is that you turn gently toward your grief instead of running away from it. When you do, you'll know you're in exactly the right place.

Who is going to walk me down the aisle?

This is a question I (Fiona) often wonder about. Since my dad died when I was thirteen, I did not have any concrete plans for my wedding. Still, the thought of missing him on that special day was (and still is) huge. The special father-daughter tradition that many girls look forward to can no longer be a reality for me.

Many girls love to dream about walking down the aisle at their weddings, but if you have lost your dad, the perfect day that you imagined might seem ruined now. After your person dies, you learn that you need to view the future differently. That's as true when you think about your wedding day as it is anything else. Regardless of how old you are, you and I need to leave this piece of our futures exclusively in God's hands. We must trust that if and when the time comes, we'll be able to testify to the words of that old hymn: "All I have needed, thy hand hath provided."[4]

Choosing the person who will walk you down the aisle, or even thinking about it, is a really hard thing. Even though you're probably years away from marriage, there may be adults in your life who want to encourage you to think about this now. You might feel pressure from others about choosing someone. The thought might even make you feel a little guilty. Will you be replacing your dad? What would he think of the person you choose? External pressures like these can prompt internal pressure that leaves us worrying about the future and forgetting God's faithfulness.

On your special day, you'll be able to choose anyone who has been important in your life to walk you down the aisle. When you consider this, you'll see the greatest truth of life after loss: life with grief is what you make it. As you lean on Jesus and seek God's wisdom, you can chart your own course in your schoolwork, your friendships, and yes, even your path down the aisle someday. You don't have to do it the way everyone else does.

PRAYER AND SCRIPTURE

God, I'll be honest. I thought my grief would eventually go away. I've wanted to be done with feeling this way for a long time. But as the time stretches between me and my loss, I also see that these sometimes-difficult emotions are a bridge that will always connect me to my person. Thank you for giving me the capacity to feel this deeply. I know that grief is a form of love.

God, I also see that you've been with me every step of the way. I haven't always felt it or noticed it, but your Word promises that you never abandon those you love, and I know that means me.[5] You've been there in the past. You're here now. And I need you to be with me for all the tomorrows that lie ahead. The future scares me when I think too much about it, but I know you're already there. Remind me that through all of life's changes, you'll never leave me alone. Amen.

> Praise be to the God and Father of our Lord Jesus Christ, the Father of compassion and the God of all comfort, who comforts us in all our troubles, so that we can comfort those in any trouble with the comfort we ourselves receive from God. For just as we share abundantly in the sufferings of Christ, so also our comfort abounds through Christ.
>
> 2 CORINTHIANS 1:3-5

Someday I'll be older than he was when he died. That's weird.

Let's be honest. That *is* weird. Death stops time in a world where time keeps going. Your loved one's life has ended and you're still getting older, whether you've lost a friend who once was your age or you will someday be older than your dad was when he died. Some days, your person's death feels like yesterday. Other days, it's as though you look back at him or her through a rearview mirror as you drive further and further away. You speed forward, and your loved one almost vanishes in the distance.

The passage of time is probably one of the strangest elements of grief that we encounter as we live and grow around our loss. Especially if you lost a loved one "too young," the way you face time's movement is very different from those around you. You might not look forward to that birthday where you mark another year that has passed. You might feel really uncomfortable the day you graduate from high school, knowing that you've now done something your loved one never got to do.

As you sit with the awkwardness of time, go ahead and acknowledge its complexity. Loss has taught you to be grateful for each day you're given, but each day can also come with reminders of grief. Let both of those feelings sit together in your mind and heart, and, if you're able, share them with someone you trust. When you engage your grief honestly like this, you'll find that your relationship to time shifts over, well, time. The pain of years that go by will change, and its sharpness will wear away.

I don't want to think about the future anymore. Is that normal?

Yes, it's totally normal. Lots of people don't like thinking about the future after their loved one dies. Not only is it hard to imagine a world without your person in it, but it's also hard to look forward to a future that's now been entirely changed by loss.

There is actually real value in the old cliché "Live one day at a time," and we encourage you to do that as long as you need to. Focus on the day before you, or the next few hours if that's all you can handle. Don't commit to lots of future plans. Keep your options open. Many people long for the familiarity of routines and systems and structure after loss because the future's ambiguity looks scary. As much as you're able, embrace small-scale routines and leave the bigger decision-making about tomorrow until tomorrow.

Jesus told his followers, "Don't worry about tomorrow, for tomorrow will bring its own worries. Today's trouble is enough for today."[6] He knew that thinking too much about the future would overwhelm his friends. They couldn't control it, and they didn't know what it held. So Jesus kindly invited them to stick close to him in the present and leave their concerns about the future to him. Jesus invites you and me to do the same thing. Knowing this, we can let even our dislike of the future rest safely in his hands.

As you commit to living fully in this day, you may find that your fears about the future ease a little. Trusting God with your present moment grows the muscles that allow you to lift your eyes and look toward the future over time too. Be open to the idea that the way your posture is now may not be the way you always face your future.

How do I handle holidays now?

If you've lost a family member, holidays can be really difficult to face. Like most situations, we encourage you to make a plan, keep expectations low, and go slowly with space to change your mind in the moment if you need to. When it comes to holidays, though, it can also help to create space to remember your person.

Many of us have specific holiday memories attached to the person we lost. Whether your grandpa always read the Christmas story on Christmas Eve or your favorite aunt brought apple cider at Thanksgiving every year, your memories of holidays are linked to these people. Since your love for them continues after their death, you can feel free to remember them in a special way at the holidays.

If the loss was recent or you need privacy, carve out a little space before, during, or after the holiday to remember on your own or with one or two trusted people. Think about your person, recalling special memories of the past. Thank God for your person's life and acknowledge that you miss them in this season. Remember all the ways that your person made the holiday special.

Then bring that person into your holiday in a way that is meaningful to you. Volunteer to bring the cider. Ask your grandmother to teach you to carve the turkey. Offer to read the Christmas story for the little kids in the family, as though your person has passed on the baton to you. Thank God for your person's life during the prayer before the meal. Write a letter to your person after the holiday is over to grieve and capture the new memories that you've made with them in mind. As much as you're able, encourage your family members to participate with you. Grieving, remembering, and celebrating together can draw your family closer, offering each of you vital support during a tough time of the year.

I've noticed that my friend group has changed in the time since my person's death. I'm not sure what to think about that.

After a loved one's death, lots of people swarm around to help and offer their sympathy. You probably got lots of "thoughts and prayers" after your person died, and you may have received a lot of care—texts, hugs, and notes—from your friends too. Over time, though, many people discover that their friendships begin to shift. Some relationships you'd hoped would stick around begin to fade. Others that seemed more like acquaintances grow closer. These changes can feel like more loss, and they often don't happen right away but over time.

While we want to assure you that it's normal for your friend group

IN THEIR OWN WORDS: EMILY'S STORY

My grandpa passed away in December 2022. It was one of the hardest losses I've ever had. He was a huge role model in my life. He taught me to be strong in difficult situations; he taught me bravery in hard times; and, most of all, he led me closer to Jesus! I loved every time I spent with him.

Since his passing, I've been sad because I miss him and his presence here on earth but also happy because he's in no pain. I'll see him again in heaven. He was the biggest Christlike person I've ever met; he led me closer to Jesus. I'm forever grateful for that. My granddad is such a big inspiration in my life, and his passing makes me want to be a bigger inspiration to other people.

—Emily, age 16, whose grandfather died three months prior

to change through the years, we also know that it probably hurts. Especially if you're feeling abandoned by these people, the pain of shifting relationships just adds to your grief. Share your feelings with a trusted adult and face that grief honestly.

Then, as you have the energy, focus on the people who have arrived in your life and those who have stuck with you through the hard stuff. The book of Proverbs tells us that "a brother is born for a time of adversity."[7] God births some relationships in your life specifically to care for you when you need it most. Look around you and make note of these friends. In the midst of so many goodbyes, these people are God's gift to you.

Some of the sweetest friendships we've made have come from our time of loss. People who showed up and treated us as "normal" when we felt anything but. People who weren't afraid to see us cry or who kept texting even if we turned down invitations to hang out. We all need both new and old relationships as we grow up through adolescence to adulthood. We're convinced that God will give you exactly what you need in this season of growth and change.

I used to have a brother, but now I don't. How do I answer questions about my family?

Some of the most awkward moments of our loss have been those moments when someone asked about our family. Suddenly it becomes very hard to answer simple questions like "How many siblings do you have?" or "Where does your dad work?" because the answers are so complicated. These questions can bring up sensitive emotions that you don't want to talk about or invite further uncomfortable questions.

We've had to learn many different ways to talk to people about our family. If you're making small talk with someone you probably won't see again, it's fine to just refer to your person in the present as if they were still there. For example, if the UPS man says, "Can you give this package to your dad?," you probably don't need to launch into an explanation of why he's unable to accept the box. You can simply say, "Sure!" Why complicate the conversation if you don't need to?

However, this isn't something you should do in all interactions. Just as you are getting used to life without your person, you need to get used to talking about them. In my life, it is easier to answer questions about my dad now than it was a few years ago. Here are some questions and answers that can help you in these situations:

WHERE DOES YOUR PARENT WORK?

In cases like this, I (Fiona) like to use the past tense to answer. I might say, "He *used to* work at [insert his workplace here]." It is a subtle hint to the person I'm talking to that my dad has died without actually saying it. It can be very hard to talk about your person dying, so something simple like using the past tense can help you ease yourself into it.

HOW MANY SIBLINGS DO YOU HAVE?

When answering questions like this, I like to combine the fact that my person has died with another statement. You might say, "My brother died, so now I have two sisters and a little brother." Answering in this way can help you state the fact that you have lost a family member while also continuing the conversation in a different direction. Death isn't something you should avoid talking about but framing it like this can help make it less awkward.

ARE YOUR PARENTS COMING?

With questions like this, I like to reply, "Yeah, my mom is coming." Instead of referring to both parents or multiple siblings as a group, you can name the one (or ones) who will be present.

As with most things in grief, practice makes progress. Over time, it will get easier to talk about your family, and you'll find your own unique ways of describing this group of people you call your own. You are the gatekeeper of your life story, and we trust you'll find the right words to tell that story as the months and years go by.

P.S. GOD
LOVES YOU

As I (Clarissa) sit writing this, our country is grieving another school shooting. Three students and three school staff died yesterday, and even though I live 1,000 miles away in quiet New England, there's a heaviness that fills this day.

When I think about the pervasiveness of sin and the brokenness of this world, I'll admit, I get mad. I get angry that all is not as it should be. My heart aches for students who have seen more than their eyes should see at their age, who have had to grow up too fast because of violence or pain. My heart hurts for you as you slog through grief you never wanted. I cry out with the psalmist, "How long, O LORD? Will you forget [us] forever?"[1]

It brings me a lot of comfort that the writer of the Psalms often felt the way I do. The phrase "How long?" shows up in the Psalms over a dozen times, which tells me that it's a good question to keep asking.[2] Like the woman who kept pestering the judge in Jesus' parable, we're invited by God to persistently and passionately bug him with our prayers—lamenting injustice, sorrow, and pain.[3] We can and should keep telling God urgently what's wrong, what we need, and how we hope he'll fix things. Today, as I scroll through news about the school shooting, I'm doing just that. *God, stop this terrible violence. Heavenly Father, bring justice and wipe away our tears. Lord Jesus, come quickly and make all things new.*

One thing is certain: Psalm 23's "valley of the shadow of death" is real.[4] Life is hard. Sometimes the mountains of hardship surround us, enclosing us in the valley of suffering. Sometimes death seems to cast a dark shadow over everything. It can be hard to believe that, in the middle of all of this trouble, God is still good and strong and capable and loving. More than that, it can be hard to believe that God takes any interest in you. You're just one person in a world full of difficulties. How could he possibly notice you?

IT'S A SCARY WORLD OUT THERE

A few months later, as I (Fiona) sat editing this chapter, our country was grieving another mass shooting, this time a little closer to home. Eighteen people were killed and thirteen wounded at a bowling alley and a bar in Maine. Hearing of these violent shootings happening at schools and other normal public places can make us afraid to go out and live our lives. All this violence, sadness, and death in the world makes us fearful for ourselves and for others. If you're wondering if God even notices you, the fear can even increase.

While grief is a very personal thing and affects each of us differently, grief is also universal. Whether a musician you love dies and won't be making music anymore, a favorite influencer succumbs to cancer, or your school steps up its security in response to a school shooting, your life is different when someone dies—even somebody you don't know in real life. All death touches us all.

Just like in an ecosystem, we were made to live in relation to the things and people around us. When one species suffers, the whole system feels it. The book of Matthew tells us that when Jesus was crucified, the earth responded in grief. The sky went black, the ground shook, and stones split in half.[5] The Creator died, and all of creation felt it. Those cries of "How long, O Lord?" can sometimes get pretty desperate. Each death can make you feel a little more vulnerable and afraid.

But Jesus offers us another option. Instead of being afraid, we know these things happen due to the brokenness caused by sin—and we know Jesus has conquered them. We don't need to fear that sin and sadness will reign in our lives or in the world because we know that he has defeated them both.

Sure, you might be thinking, *I* know *that I don't have to be afraid, but Jesus' message doesn't make me* feel *any different.* That is totally normal! Just because we know something to be true doesn't mean that it's going to change the way we act.

So what does it look like to actually apply this truth to the way we live our lives? Well, I have to tell you that it takes a lot of conscious decisions. Satan wants our brain's default to be fear because that makes us distrust God. He is whispering in our ears the same thing he asked Eve in the Garden: "Does God *really* know what's best for you?"[6] Because of this we have to be mindful of how we let fear affect our lives. We can hear about school shootings and be afraid to go back to school. We can lose someone in a car crash and not want to get in a car again. But we don't have to let this fear control us.

One day, conversation in my English class veered down a rabbit trail. Scary and sad headlines had us all worried as we saw bad things happening, and my teacher told us something that will stick with me forever. He said, "I have a lot of concerns, but I'm not afraid of anything."

Concern and fear are two very different things. Fear is a knee-jerk reaction to bad things that threaten us. It makes us tremble every time we leave the comfort of our house. Concern, on the other hand, takes intentional thought. It is productive and freeing. It leads us to think rationally about situations and take precautions, and it frees us to live our lives fully. The hymn "What a Friend We Have in Jesus" speaks beautifully to this: "O what peace we often forfeit, O what needless pain we bear, all because we do not carry everything to God in prayer!"[7] We often bear "needless pain" without thinking because we haven't made it a habit to bring these issues to God.

My teacher told us to create an altar in our minds where we could offer all our fears to God. I encourage you to do the same thing. Imagine a place where you take your grief and fears and tell God, "I don't want these to control my life. I want you to." While it is hard to step away from the fight-or-flight reaction to fear, we can learn to intentionally offer everything to the God who cares for us. We can do this because, as Scripture assures us, God is always paying attention to our cries, even when we can't imagine he'd have time amid all the other troubles of this world.[8]

HEARD, KNOWN, SEEN

A funny thing happens every time I (Clarissa) go to the mall. Regardless of whether I'm alone or not, every time I hear someone call out, "Mom!" I turn to see if the person is talking to me. After being a mother for almost two decades, I respond to my title pretty quickly—even if the person isn't one of my children!

It might be hard to believe, but in the middle of life's crazy noise, God still turns when he hears you call his name. Every time you desire his attention, he's already listening. Every time you wish he'd look, he's already got his eyes fixed on you. Like a mom in a crowded mall, God perks up his ears when he hears your voice.

God's attention toward you is even better, though. When that voice calls out, "Mom!" at the mall, I quickly realize it isn't my child.

I look around, identify the speaker, and move on my way. My brain registers, *She's not talking to me*, and my attention shifts elsewhere. I'm not needed there. God *never* does that with you. Never. The Gospel of John tells us that Jesus recognizes each of us as his own and stands ready to respond.[9] Even when it feels like life's chaos drowns out your one small voice, God is listening and poised to act. We know this is true because God sent Jesus to meet our greatest need.

If you wonder if God is listening, you need look no further than the person of Jesus. The Gospel of John tells us that, as the world groaned under the weight of sin, our heavenly Father sent his Son to live and die as one of us.[10] Jesus' arrival on this planet signaled above all else that God is listening and that his love pursues us to the greatest lengths—through sin, death, and Satan's captivating deception.

Without Jesus, we were forever dead in our sin. We could not live a perfect life. We had no chance of resisting the devil's trap. But then, without us doing anything for God—before we had done anything good at all—Jesus chose to take the price of our sin upon himself. In our world, it seems ridiculous to give up your life for someone who hasn't done anything for you. But Jesus loves us so much that he was willing to die in order to call us his own. Through his death, Jesus conquered death forever—your person's, yours, and mine.

Jesus' death gives us a way to know God and to be close to him. Even in our darkest nights, our hardest times, and the worst days of our lives, Jesus' death and resurrection remind us that God is always listening. He never has abandoned us, and he never will. When it seems like nothing could get worse, Jesus' death and resurrection offer us a bright hope. He won't leave us in our suffering. Through Jesus' death and resurrection, God redeemed the world and has set us on a path toward restoration and eternal joy in his presence.

We do not know the day or time that Jesus will return, but we are assured that in God's perfect timing, he will make all things right. One day Jesus will come again and renew the heavens and the earth. He will gather together all those who have been faithful to him, and they will be joined with him in his glorious presence for eternity. Revelation 21:4 says that when that day comes, "'He will wipe every tear from their eyes. There will be no more death' or mourning or crying or pain, for the old order of things has passed away."

As grieving Christians, this offers us a beautiful and hopeful picture for the future. When Jesus comes again, our grief will be turned to joy and our tears replaced with laughter. Though we suffer now as we participate in Christ's death, we will also one day experience his victorious resurrection.[11] In this life, we will glimpse little pieces of that victory, but Jesus has promised to raise us all up into his full glory. Until then, we can run the race ahead of us with Jesus and grief as our companions, looking forward to the glory he has set before us.

Jesus told his followers, "My purpose is to give [you] a rich and satisfying life."[12] When he said this, he didn't mean mansions or expensive shoes, fame, or popularity. God offers us so much more—"the incomparable riches of his grace, expressed in his kindness to us."[13] This is a "now and not yet" kind of grace—a grace we tap into now and will know in fullness when we meet Jesus face-to-face.

The grace Jesus offers covers our sin and saves us from eternal separation from God. The grace he offers comforts us in our grief with the deep understanding of a friend who knows what it means to hurt. And, most glorious of all, the amazing grace Jesus offers will keep us safe through everything we face because, one day, that grace will lead us home.

Your grief has shaped your life, just as your love for your person has shaped your life. You, like Jesus, bear scars of the hard things that have happened to you. But you were made for so much more than a scarred life. You were made for glory. As you face grief head-on and learn to live beside it, Jesus' resurrection manifests in your life. Every time you grieve honestly and take a step forward into your new life, you testify to this resurrection power. You confirm that God's promises are true. We know this is a life you never would have chosen, but you're doing it anyway. We're so proud of you. Keep at it. Keep going. Whether or not you can see it now, a glorious future awaits you.

APPENDIX

NUMBERS AND WEBSITES
YOU SHOULD KNOW

THEHOPELINE

CHAT: Find live Christian grief support at www.thehopeline.com.

NATIONAL EATING DISORDERS ASSOCIATION

VISIT: https://www.nationaleatingdisorders.org/get-help/

CALL:
ANAD Helpline: 888-375-7767
National Alliance for Eating Disorders Helpline: 866-662-1235
Diabulimia Helpline: 425-985-3635

If you are in crisis, call or text Suicide and Crisis Lifeline: 988
[Spanish speaking services and for Deaf & Hard of Hearing] or text
Crisis Text Line: "HOME" to 741-741 [Spanish speaking services].

SUICIDE AND CRISIS LIFELINE

CALL or TEXT: 988

OUR GRIEF PLAYLIST

Music has played a big role in our lives with loss. Here are a few playlists we've found helpful for the many expressions of our grief. Add them to one of your own playlists or check them out at https://open.spotify.com/user/outerdock.

FOR WHEN YOU NEED REASSURANCE OF GOD'S LOVE

1. "Firm Foundation (He Won't)" by Maverick City Music
2. "Lord, I Need You" by Matt Maher
3. "Undeniable" by TobyMac
4. "I Won't Let You Go" by Switchfoot and Lauren Daigle
5. "We've Got This Hope" by Ellie Holcomb
6. "Reckless Love" by Cory Asbury
7. "Who You Say I Am" by Hillsong Worship
8. "Nail Scarred Hands" by Dante Bowe
9. "Heart of God" by Zach Williams
10. "Come as You Are" by Crowder

FOR WHEN YOU WANT TO SMILE

1. "Happy" by Pharrell Williams
2. "Firework" by Katy Perry
3. "Can't Stop the Feeling!" by Justin Timberlake
4. "Sir Duke" by Stevie Wonder
5. "Drag Me Down" by One Direction
6. "Everywhere I Go" by Tim Timmons
7. "I'm Good" by Tim Bowman Jr.
8. "Lovely Day" by Bill Withers
9. "Beautiful Day" by U2
10. "Best Day of My Life" by American Authors

FOR WHEN YOU HOPE FOR THE FUTURE

1. "Make It Through" by Leanna Crawford
2. "King of Kings" by Hillsong Worship
3. "Brighter Days" by Blessing Offor
4. "Hymn of Heaven" by Phil Wickham
5. "Rainbow" by Kacey Musgraves
6. "Stuck in a Moment You Can't Get Out Of" by U2
7. "This Is Home" by Switchfoot
8. "Radiant Reason" by Kings Kaleidoscope
9. "The World You Want" by Switchfoot
10. "Live It Well" by Switchfoot

NOVELS TO HELP YOU PROCESS LOSS

LITTLE WOMEN BY LOUISA MAY ALCOTT

Author Louisa May Alcott knew what it was like to live with loss. After returning from her work as a Civil War nurse, Alcott wrote this semiautobiographical story of a family who faced the death of a sibling and learned to live again in grief's shadow. While many movie adaptations of this book exist, we recommend actually reading it because the March family's deep faith in God's goodness and care shines forth on every page. It's a theme that's often missed in the film versions but essential to understanding how Alcott believed we could endure loss and find hope in the midst of despair.

THE REMARKABLE JOURNEY OF COYOTE SUNRISE BY DAN GEMEINHART

This book was our first family read-aloud after the loss of our dad. I (Clarissa) bought it because it was about a girl whose mom and sisters had died, but I had no idea how integral its themes would be in setting the course for our grieving. Get ready to take a wild ride with a father actively running away from his grief and his daughter discovering how she can express hers. In the early weeks after Rob's death, our family talked about this book every night—hashing out what healthy grieving looked like, exploring how we would express our own grief. It was the perfect "show, don't tell" novel for us. I suspect you'll read it and see yourself somewhere in the story.

THE TIGER RISING BY KATE DiCAMILLO

Like Coyote Sunrise, Rob Horton is fighting despair after the death of his mother. The narrative is thick with metaphor as we see Rob face and release his own deep grief as he fights to save a caged tiger in the woods. This book allows you to observe a character sort out his feelings, learning that each one offers wisdom as he charts a new course for his life.

AFTER THE RIVER THE SUN BY DIA CALHOUN

Set in the stunning Methow Valley of Washington State, this novel in verse tells the story of a boy whose parents have died in a rafting accident. Courage runs through this book as a dominant theme. Watch Eckhart avoid his sadness, face it, and learn to live alongside it in page after page of beautiful poetry. Showing up to your grief takes lots of courage, and *After the River the Sun* shows you that you can be brave *and* honest in the face of loss too.

THE BIG WAVE BY PEARL S. BUCK

This classic short story is set in Japan in a small village destroyed by a tsunami. While the other books we've recommended focus much of their attention on the person who has lost a loved one, *The Big Wave* not only offers insight on the grieving person but also a glimpse into the hearts of those who comfort us. If you've struggled to feel connection with those who are trying to help you, this book can offer some validation. It can also remind you of the genuine help and care that are available to sustain us through grief's hardest days. *The Big Wave* reminds us that we don't need to—and can't—do this hard thing all alone.

MOVIES THAT HONOR LOSS

Whether you're looking for a tearjerker or you just want to watch a movie that makes sense in your mixed-up world, these movies create space for loss by telling stories of grief and hope.

We always recommend that you read a review before watching the movie to make sure it's right for where you're at. Check out reliable reviews at pluggedin.com and commonsensemedia.org.

UP (2009, PG)

This award-winning Pixar movie is all about finding new life after loss. The main character, Carl Fredricksen, has experienced sadness throughout his life—first when his pregnant wife miscarries and then, later, when she becomes ill and dies. Still, life holds so much hope for Carl, if he has the eyes to see it. Watch this movie when you need to remember that God has good things in store for you, not in isolation from your grief but in and through it.

INSIDE OUT (2015, PG)

Another great Pixar film, *Inside Out* doesn't talk about death, but it does offer an accurate picture of what it feels like to have lots of emotions swirling around inside of you. Journey through life with the characters Joy, Sadness, Anger, Fear, and Disgust to see how all your feelings have value and important things to say. Watch this movie when you need validation that God created all of you, that your complex emotional makeup is his design and gift to you.

MY GIRL (1991, PG)

Vada has been around death her whole life: her mother died when she was born, and she encounters it daily in the funeral parlor that her father runs. However, she struggles with the reality of grieving in a place where dying seems like no big deal. Watch this classic nineties rom-com if you're struggling to process all the confusing feelings that come with losing a family member or a friend and building a new life afterward. If you don't seem to feel the same as others around you, *My Girl* offers reassurance that you can face grief in the way that's right for you.

WE BOUGHT A ZOO (2011, PG)

People do crazy things after their person dies. When his wife dies, Benjamin Mee does the craziest—he buys a dilapidated zoo! Follow the Mee family as they wrestle with the changes that loss brings, the many ways different family members grieve, and the pull of life forward toward beauty and new possibilities. Watch this movie with a box of tissues when you're ready to feel the feels and smile through your tears.

WE ARE MARSHALL (2006, PG)

This classic football movie features Matthew McConaughey as a football coach hired to resurrect a college team after a terrible accident that kills 75 people—including many of the team's players and coaching staff. Cinematic game moments are punctuated with displays of real grief—from the anxiety that comes after loss to survivor's guilt to the anger we feel when others don't understand what we've been through. If your school or community has suffered a shared loss, this movie can give you space to express your collective grief and hope to rebuild.

YOUR GRIEF RELIEF TOOL KIT

Every carpenter has a box of tools for woodworking projects. Every hiker packs ten essentials in her backpack for a day out in the mountains. As you move about your life with grief, consider making your own grief relief tool kit. Keep a kit in your locker, in your school bag, and/or in your bedroom so you have helpful items at the ready when you're feeling a wave of loss coming on.

Grab a gallon ziplock bag, pencil case, or other bag to keep your kit together when you're on the go. (Hint: If an adult says, "Let me know how I can help," give them this list of items and ask them to grab them at the store for you.)

Be sure to include:

FOR YOUR BODY

- A travel-size pack of tissues
- A travel-size pack of facial cleansing wipes
- A tube of lip balm
- An individual-size protein snack that's low in sugar (jerky sticks, nuts, or individual nut butters work great!)
- A small sugary pick-me-up (We love Snickers!)

FOR YOUR MIND AND HEART

- A rubber band, fidget toy, or deck of cards to keep your hands busy
- A small notepad for jotting thoughts down
- Your favorite pen (We love Pilot G2 gel pens!)
- A verse written on a note card that encourages your heart
- A picture of you with your person
- A small container of hand lotion in a favorite scent that grounds and calms you

CREATING A MEMORY BOOK

While it's great to have pictures on your phone, we really love the idea of creating a special place to keep memories of your person. This creative work separates you from the habit of "zombie scrolling" on your phone—yes, that's what researchers actually call that mindless swiping we do!—and gives you a sense of agency (or power) over the shaping of your story with your person.

If you're the creative type, print those photos from your phone or collect photos of your person and place them in a journal, scrapbook, or photo album. Add ticket stubs from shows or games you attended together. Include the notes he passed you in class or the Christmas card she sent you with her signature on the inside. Whatever little bits of paraphernalia you've got, stick them in there! When we lose someone we love, every item can be precious.

Alongside these items, write a few short words to summarize the experience or include a memory of your person. As time wears on, we often forget details, and this conscious remembering can be a helpful way to get those memories out of your brain and onto paper so they don't get lost. Add to your memory book over time as you find other items or as old memories resurface. Let your book become a living testimony to your love for your person and your relationship with them.

Low on the creative juices? You can still create a depository of memories! Whether you grab a shoebox and fill it with old letters and pictures or you use a website like Snapfish (snapfish.com) or Shutterfly (shutterfly.com) to make a photo book, you can collect the memories that are precious to you and keep them in a single spot. Some apps like Chatbooks and Mixbook even allow you to create these items on your phone!

When you're particularly lonely for your person or you want to celebrate their life, you can pull out this collection of memories and remember the love that remains even after death.

VERSES TO GET YOU THROUGH

Even when I walk through the darkest valley, I will not be afraid, for you are close beside me. Your rod and your staff protect and comfort me.

PSALM 23:4, NLT

Don't be afraid, for I am with you. Don't be discouraged, for I am your God. I will strengthen you and help you. I will hold you up with my victorious right hand.

ISAIAH 41:10, NLT

I will not forget you! See, I have engraved you on the palms of my hands.

ISAIAH 49:15-16

For the LORD your God is living among you. He is a mighty savior. He will take delight in you with gladness. With his love, he will calm all your fears. He will rejoice over you with joyful songs.

ZEPHANIAH 3:17, NLT

Now is your time of grief, but I will see you again and you
will rejoice, and no one will take away your joy. . . . I have
told you these things, so that in me you may have peace.
In this world you will have trouble. But take heart! I have
overcome the world.

JOHN 16:22, 33

Who shall separate us from the love of Christ? Shall trouble
or hardship or persecution or famine or nakedness or danger
or sword? . . . No, in all these things we are more than
conquerors through him who loved us. For I am convinced
that neither death nor life, neither angels nor demons,
neither the present nor the future, nor any powers, neither
height nor depth, nor anything else in all creation, will be
able to separate us from the love of God that is in Christ
Jesus our Lord.

ROMANS 8:35, 37-39

ACKNOWLEDGMENTS

We are grateful to Andrew Wolgemuth, who saw the value for teenagers in a gospel-centered grief book all their own. Our deepest thanks to the fantastic team at Tyndale—Linda Howard, Talia Messina, Danika Kelly, Lisanne Kaufmann, Mary Mayo, Natalie Wierenga, Jackie Nuñez, and Jen Phelps—who brought our idea to life.

The book of Proverbs reminds us that in many counselors there is wisdom. Such has been the gracious task of Heather Beville, Lisa Clay, Chelsea Erickson, and Jason Lawrenz, who reviewed the early draft. Thank you for your parenting insight and professional acumen. You have made our words better.

Thank you to Elise Boros for your clear, wise words and to Camille Fisher for scouring bookstores in search of great teen book covers. Thank you, Anna Meade Harris, for parenting wisdom that has lit the way before us.

We are especially grateful to the young people who shared their honest experiences with loss. Brianna, Emerson, Emily, Libby, Mac, Meredith, Rachel, and Violet, your lives are a testimony to God's resurrection goodness. May you always know his delight and care over you.

NOTES

WELCOME
1. Jeremiah 29:11-13.
2. See 1 Kings 19:11-12.
3. Stuart Townend and Dustin Kensrue, "Rejoice," 2013, https://www.stuarttownend.co.uk/song/rejoice/.
4. Revelation 19:11.
5. See Colossians 1:13-14.

CHAPTER 1: IN YOUR BODY
1. See John 1:14.
2. Litsa Williams, "Grief Theory 101: The Dual Process Model of Grief," What's Your Grief?, September 23, 2014, https://whatsyourgrief.com/dual-process-model-of-grief/.
3. Peter Wehner, "Why Is Jesus Still Wounded after His Resurrection?" *New York Times*, April 3, 2021, https://www.nytimes.com/2021/04/03/opinion/christ-resurrection-easter.html.
4. "Hunger and Appetite," GI Society, April 1, 2020, https://badgut.org/information-centre/a-z-digestive-topics/hunger-and-appetite/.
5. "Hunger and Appetite," GI Society.
6. Fahham Asghar et al., "Telogen Effluvium: A Review of the Literature," *Cureus* 12, no. 5 (May 27, 2020): e8320, https://doi.org/10.7759/cureus.8320.
7. Christopher Winter, "Choosing the Best Temperature for Sleep," HuffPost, last modified October 9, 2013, https://www.huffpost.com/entry/best-temperature-for-sleep_b_3705049.
8. Psalm 18:28, GW.
9. Lisa M. Shulman, *Before and after Loss: A Neurologist's Perspective on Loss, Grief, and Our Brain* (Baltimore: Johns Hopkins University Press, 2018), 56.
10. Silas Weir Mitchell, "The Case of George Dedlow," *Atlantic*, July 1866, https://www.theatlantic.com/magazine/archive/1866/07/the-case-of-george-dedlow/308771/.

11. C. S. Lewis, *A Grief Observed* (New York: HarperOne, 2001), 61.
12. Srini Pillay, "The 'Thinking' Benefits of Doodling," Harvard Health, December 15, 2016, https://www.health.harvard.edu/blog/the-thinking-benefits-of-doodling -2016121510844.
13. Hui-Ling Lai and Marion Good, "Music Improves Sleep Quality in Older Adults," *Journal of Advanced Nursing* 49, no. 3 (February 2005): 234–244, https://onlinelibrary.wiley.com/doi/10.1111/j.1365-2648.2004.03281.x.
14. "Stress Relief from Laughter? It's No Joke," Mayo Clinic, September 22, 2023, https://www.mayoclinic.org/healthy-lifestyle/stress-management/in-depth/stress -relief/art-20044456.
15. "Stress Relief from Laughter?," Mayo Clinic.
16. Imke Kirste et al., "Is Silence Golden? Effects of Auditory Stimuli and Their Absence on Adult Hippocampal Neurogenesis," *Brain Structure and Function* 220 (2015): 1221–1228, https://www.researchgate.net/publication/259110014_Is_silence _golden_Effects_of_auditory_stimuli_and_their_absence_on_adult_hippocampal _neurogenesis.

CHAPTER 2: NUTS & BOLTS
1. Psalm 139:16; Proverbs 19:21.
2. *con* = with, *dolor* = grief, for those of you taking Spanish class.
3. Psalm 148:2, 11-12.
4. Ecclesiastes 9:2.
5. Philippians 1:23-24, NLT.
6. See Matthew 26:36-45.

CHAPTER 3: ALL THE FEELS
1. *Inside Out*, directed by Pete Docter and Ronnie Del Carmen (Emeryville, CA: Disney Pixar, 2015), https://www.imdb.com/title/tt2096673/quotes/?ref_=tt_trv_qu.
2. Dr. Jenn Hardy, Instagram post, June 13, 2021, https://www.instagram.com/p /CQFLg78Ds-j/?igshid=MDJmNzVkMjY.
3. Genesis 1:31.
4. Genesis 1:26, NLT.
5. Kenneth J. Doka and Terry L. Martin, *Grieving beyond Gender: Understanding the Ways Men and Women Mourn* (New York: Routledge, 2010).
6. See John 11:35.
7. See Matthew 21:12-13.
8. See Matthew 26:38.
9. Colossians 1:15.
10. Ephesians 4:26, ESV.
11. Psalm 7:11, ESV.
12. See 1 Peter 1:7.
13. Lily Collins, *Unfiltered: No Shame, No Regrets, Just Me* (New York: HarperCollins, 2017), 127.
14. See John 10:11-16.
15. Alain Romeyer and Marie-France Bouissou, "Assessment of Fear Reactions in Domestic Sheep, and Influence of Breed and Rearing Conditions," *Applied Animal*

Behaviour Science 34, no. 1–2 (July 1992): 93–119, https://www.sciencedirect.com
/science/article/abs/pii/S0168159105800607.

16. Isaiah 41:10.
17. Litsa Williams, "Grief Theory 101: The Dual Process Model of Grief," What's Your
Grief? September 23, 2014, https://whatsyourgrief.com/dual-process-model-of-grief/.
18. Emily P. Freeman, "152: Say Words with Your Out Loud Voice," Emily P. Freeman,
accessed December 21, 2023, https://emilypfreeman.com/podcast/152/.
19. Genesis 50:20.
20. See Psalm 139:16-17.
21. Philippians 4:12-13.

CHAPTER 4: THE BIG MAN UPSTAIRS

1. Timothy Keller, *The Reason for God: Belief in an Age of Skepticism* (New York:
Penguin Books, 2018), 245.
2. "Grief, Grieving," *Baker's Evangelical Dictionary of Biblical Theology*, ed. Walter A.
Elwell (Grand Rapids, MI: Baker Books, 1996), Bible Study Tools, https://www
.biblestudytools.com/dictionaries/bakers-evangelical-dictionary/grief-grieving.html.
3. John 9:3, MSG.
4. See Matthew 5:45.
5. John 9:3, MSG.
6. See Romans 8:28.
7. See Colossians 1:15.
8. See Ecclesiastes 3:11.
9. See Luke 16:19-31.
10. N. T. Wright, *The Resurrection of the Son of God* (Minneapolis: Fortress Press, 2003), 31.
11. C. S. Lewis, *The Collected Letters of C. S. Lewis: Narnia, Cambridge, and Joy 1950–
1963*, ed. Walter Hooper, vol. 3 (New York: HarperCollins, 2007), 1430.
12. See Luke 23:42-43.
13. See 2 Peter 3:9.
14. Thomas Merton, *Dialogues with Silence: Prayers & Drawings*, ed. Jonathan Montaldo
(San Francisco: HarperSanFrancisco, 2001), 57.
15. See Hebrews 10:25.
16. 1 John 4:19.
17. See Isaiah 66:13.
18. See Isaiah 49:16.
19. See Luke 15:20.
20. See Revelation 3:20.
21. Romans 5:3-5, NLT.
22. Isaiah 55:8-9.

CHAPTER 5: WHEN GRIEF IS OLD NEWS

1. "Cold Food Storage Chart," FoodSafety.gov, September 19, 2023, https://www
.foodsafety.gov/food-safety-charts/cold-food-storage-charts.
2. See Romans 8:22.
3. Dennis Klass, Phyllis R. Silverman, and Steven L. Nickman, *Continuing Bonds: New
Understandings of Grief* (New York: Routledge, 1996).

4. Thomas O. Chisholm, "Great Is Thy Faithfulness," 1923.
5. See Deuteronomy 31:8.
6. Matthew 6:34, NLT.
7. Proverbs 17:17.

P.S. GOD LOVES YOU
1. Psalm 13:1, ESV.
2. Visit biblegateway.com and type in "How long." You'll be amazed to see how often biblical characters ask this question!
3. See Luke 18:1-8.
4. Psalm 23:4, ESV.
5. See Matthew 27:45-53.
6. See Genesis 3:1-5.
7. Joseph Medlicott Scriven, "What a Friend We Have in Jesus," 1855, https://hymnary .org/text/what_a_friend_we_have_in_jesus_all_our_s.
8. See Psalm 34:15.
9. See John 10:14-18.
10. See John 3:16.
11. See 1 Peter 4:13.
12. John 10:10, NLT.
13. Ephesians 2:7.

ABOUT THE AUTHORS

CLARISSA MOLL is an award-winning writer and podcaster who helps bereaved people find flourishing after loss. Clarissa's writing appears in *Christianity Today*, The Gospel Coalition, *RELEVANT*, Modern Loss, *Grief Digest*, and more. She cohosted *Christianity Today's Surprised by Grief* podcast and produces *Christianity Today's* flagship news podcast, *The Bulletin*. She holds a master's degree from Trinity Evangelical Divinity School and is a frequent guest on podcasts and radio shows. Find her on Instagram at @mollclarissa or at clarissamoll.com.

FIONA MOLL is a college student whose dad died when she was 13 years old. Fiona's research interests include biology and the natural world, a place that brought her comfort and hope as she processed her loss as a young teenager. She loves hiking, reading, and spending time with her family. *Hurt Help Hope* is her first book.

Also from Clarissa Moll

Whether you've lost someone dear to you or you're supporting a loved one as they mourn, you can learn to walk with grief. In her debut book, Clarissa offers her powerful personal narrative as well as honest, practical wisdom that will gently guide you toward flourishing amid your own loss.

Your Feelings
Aren't Weird

THE GOOD, THE NOT-SO-GOOD,

ALL THE FEELS
FOR TEENS
AND THE UTTERLY CONFUSING

ELIZABETH
LAING THOMPSON

"Part workbook, part self-help guide, part Bible study, this handbook is geared toward those who experience big feelings and could use some support navigating the challenges that come with this territory. . . . Overwhelmed teens can find validation in this faith-based guide."
—*Kirkus Reviews*